Illustrator:
Howard Chaney

Editor:
Evan D. Forbes, M.S. Ed.

Editor in Chief:
Sharon Coan, M.S. Ed.

Art Director:
Elayne Roberts

Associate Designer:
Denise Bauer

Cover Artist:
Susan Williams

Product Manager:
Phil Garcia

Imaging:
David Bennett

Acknowledgements:

HyperStudio® is a registered trademark of Roger Wagner Publishing, Inc.

ClarisWorks software and screenshots are © 1991-95 Claris Corporation. All Rights Reserved. *ClarisWorks* is a registered trademark of Claris Corporation in the U.S. and other countries.

Screen shot(s) reprinted with permission from Microsoft Corporation.

Kid Pix 2®, Copyright Brøderbund Software, Inc., 1996. All Rights Reserved.

Apple the Apple Logo and Macintosh are trademarks of Apple Computer, Inc., registered in the United States and other countries.

The Writing Center™ is a registered trademark of The Learning Company.

Publishers:
Rachelle Cracchiolo, M.S. Ed.
Mary Dupuy Smith, M.S. Ed.

INTEGRATING TECHNOLOGY INTO THE CURRICULUM

INTERMEDIATE

Author:

Mary H

D1445074

Teacher Crea...

P.O. Box 1040
Huntington Beach, CA   92647

ISBN-1-55734-934-7

Teacher Created Materials

©*1996 Teacher Created Materials, Inc.*   Made in U.S.A.

TABLE OF CONTENTS

TABLE OF CONTENTS *(cont.)*

INTRODUCTION

As the development and use of technology grows in our society, it also grows in importance in our schools. But, with the busy schedules of today's teachers, where do they find not only the time but the know-how to plan meaningful technology lessons, especially if they are not comfortable using or talking about computers? *Integrating Technology into the Curriculum* will provide solutions for technology coordinators, lab teachers, and classroom teachers who are in search of ideas that integrate technology into their curriculum.

The first part of *Integrating Technology into the Curriculum* will focus on ideas to help organize technology in your classroom. There are suggestions for scheduling, planning, and management of the one-computer and the multi-computer classrooms, as well as the computer lab. Some of the scheduling and management suggestions in this book deal with comparing fixed schedules to flexible schedules, introducing new projects, and reinforcing appropriate student behavior within the computer lab. There are suggestions for ways to individualize computer projects for students with special needs (e.g., gifted students and students with learning disabilities). Also included are ideas for joint planning and team teaching among teachers and specialists to produce the best possible student work. Appropriate assessment of technology projects can be difficult. Once you have a student product, how do you assess it? There are ideas for performance assessment, such as checklists and rubrics, as well as teacher, peer, and self-assessment ideas.

Part two of *Integrating Technology into the Curriculum* offers concrete ideas for enhancing the curriculum through student projects on the computer. Included are lessons integrating technology into language arts, math, social studies, science and health, and special areas (i.e., art, music, physical education, and foreign language). Each lesson includes a topic, subject area, appropriate grade level, lesson plan, advanced organizers for the student (if needed), and assessment recommendations for you, the teacher. Each lesson plan includes helpful tips for teaching the lesson, as well as software recommendations.

Integrating Technology into the Curriculum is an excellent resource for classroom teachers looking for ways to use technology to extend their elementary curriculum.

THE COMPUTER LAB

A very common way to arrange computers in the elementary school is organizing them into a computer lab. The computer lab is a room that has been designed for the housing and operation of a school's computers. It may be run by a computer professional who is not a teacher. Although in many schools, computer labs are a place to perform "drill and skill" activities, these labs are slowly metamorphosing into technology centers—places where multimedia projects are created, telecommunications are taking place, presentations are made, and student television broadcasts are captured on film. Computer labs have assumed a role similar to the media center, becoming a hub of school activity. Therefore, it is necessary to take some things into account when equipping a technology lab.

PHILOSOPHY

What is your school's philosophy of technology in education? Some educators feel that technology plays a very minor role, while others feel it is crucial to prepare students to operate in today's workplace. You must decide as a staff the role you feel technology should play in the lives of your students and base your technology lab on those principles.

PURPOSE

What is the purpose of technology in the education of students? Quite often teachers see computers as something extra to do once the business of learning has taken place. It is important to realize that a computer is a tool to help students and teachers accomplish something better, neater, faster, or more efficiently, not a place to play when meaningful work is done.

SOFTWARE

There is currently a debate about the presence of instructional versus productivity software. Instructional software takes a concept and extends or reinforces it. Some instructional software programs have amazing simulations and problem-solving activities, while some are no better than expensive workbooks put on the computer. Productivity software is used as a tool. It helps teachers or students create a product such as a word processed document, a piece of art, or a multimedia presentation. The activities in this book are all completed using productivity software. So . . . what do you emphasize? Certainly that will be based on your philosophy as a school, but they both have their own unique place in classroom integration.

EQUIPMENT

So, you are ready as a school to jump on the integrated technology bandwagon. What do you do if most of your equipment is outdated and cannot run much of the software you want? It is never too early to begin planning and making that shift. Begin teacher training and get your parent group's support. You would be amazed at how much you can raise with bake sales and craft fairs if you can get your parent population involved. Also, look into educational technology magazines for available grants. Technology is receiving a great deal of interest and funding right now—you just have to find it.

SCHEDULING

There are many options available when scheduling teacher slots in an elementary computer lab. The most common seems to be a fixed schedule, but flexible scheduling is becoming more popular as the use of technology increases in elementary schools. Each school has different needs. Investigate the different scheduling options open to you and choose the one that fits your school's needs best.

THE FIXED SCHEDULE

This is currently the most common scheduling method in elementary schools, where every open slot in the lab is filled with a class. This schedule repeats itself week after week. Each class in the school attends the lab a regular number of times each week.

Advantages of a Fixed Schedule:

- A fixed schedule sets a routine for the teacher and students by creating a set lab time every week.
- Fixed schedules ensure equitable distribution of lab time.
- Teachers cannot lose time slots because they forgot to sign up or there were no convenient times.

Disadvantages of a Fixed Schedule:

- Teachers are not able to sign up for more lab time for large projects if needed.
- Students may see working on the computer as just a part of their routine instead of thinking of it as a tool for its true purpose—to create a better product than they can create without it.

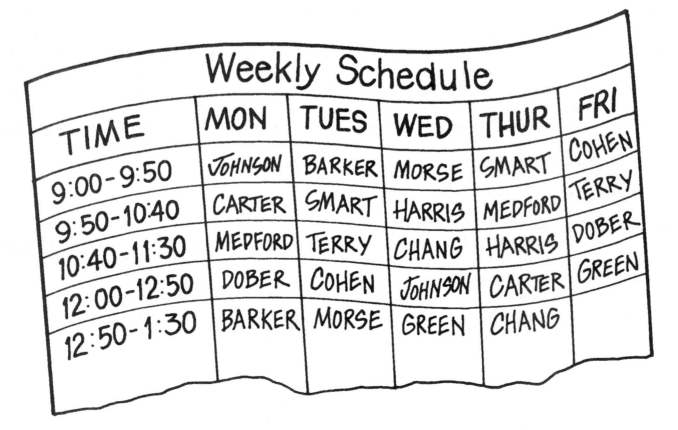

TIME	MON	TUES	WED	THUR	FRI
9:00 - 9:50	JOHNSON	BARKER	MORSE	SMART	COHEN
9:50 - 10:40	CARTER	SMART	HARRIS	MEDFORD	TERRY
10:40 - 11:30	MEDFORD	TERRY	CHANG	HARRIS	DOBER
12:00 - 12:50	DOBER	COHEN	JOHNSON	CARTER	GREEN
12:50 - 1:30	BARKER	MORSE	GREEN	CHANG	

Weekly Schedule

SCHEDULING *(cont.)*

THE FLEXIBLE SCHEDULE

Flexible scheduling is different from a fixed schedule because it changes from week to week. All of the open slots in a lab are shared among all teachers. A flexible schedule allows teachers to sign up for slots as needed, instead of being tied into a certain time slot every week. For example, if a teacher is creating a *Kid Pix* slide show as the culminating activity in a social studies unit, it may take six or more visits to the computer lab. This could spread the project out over many weeks—long past the end of the unit in the classroom. With flexible scheduling, a teacher can schedule those six slots in the lab as needed over a one- or two-week period, while the students are involved in the topic in the classroom.

Time	Monday	Tuesday	Wednesday	Thursday	Friday
9:00-9:50	Jones	Jones	Jones	Julius	Jones
9:50-10:40	Feldman	Julius	Jones	Preez	Preez
10:40-11:30	Feldman	Pittman	Pittman	Pittman	Preez
11:30-12:00	Santelli	Terry	Preez	Terry	Terry
12:00-12:50	Alexander	Terry	O'Boyle	Oxford	O'Boyle
12:50-1:40	Minter	Minter	Minter	Minter	O'Boyle
1:40-2:30	Cornell	Oxford	Oxford	Alexander	Cornell
2:30-3:10	Bryant	Bryant	Bryant	Bryant	Byrant

ADVANTAGES OF A FLEXIBLE SCHEDULE:

- Teachers have more flexibility in scheduling.
- A flexible schedule allows indepth projects to be completed in a timely manner.
- This ensures optimum use of the lab—teachers sign up for specific projects instead of looking for something to do in the lab at the last minute.
- Teachers who depend on a routine may sign up for the same time each week.

DISADVANTAGES OF A FLEXIBLE SCHEDULE:

- Students may not have time in the computer lab every single week.
- Teachers who are less comfortable in the lab may not sign up as often.
- Teachers may not get time slots that fit best into their schedules.

SCHEDULING *(cont.)*

Fixed schedules have been easily used and understood in elementary schools for years. Generally, a committee of teachers and administrators work together to place teachers into fixed weekly slots that do not conflict with their lunchtimes or special classes. There are several organizational points to keep in mind if your school is interested in switching to a flexible scheduling method. Below is a guide to help your school implement flexible scheduling.

Count the number of slots available per week in the computer lab. You can divide these by teacher, or you can divide them by grade level, giving some grade levels more slots in the lab.

For example, for a school with 40 slots per week in the computer lab, you can have lab sign-up by six-week, nine-week, or 12-week periods, depending on how your school is organized and how far ahead your teachers want to plan. (It is not recommended to schedule week by week because you run the risk of teachers putting their projects off until the end of the scheduling period and making a mad rush for lab time.) Our example will examine a school that has lab sign-up every six weeks.

Time	Monday	Tuesday	Wednesday	Thursday	Friday
9:00-9:50					
9:50-10:40					
10:40-11:30					
11:30-12:00					
12:00-12:50					
12:50-1:40					
1:40-2:30					
2:30-3:10					

If your school used this exact schedule, you would have 240 slots to offer during those six weeks (40 slots per week multiplied by six weeks).

TIME SLOT DISTRIBUTION

- You could break the distribution down by the number of teachers: If you have 24 teachers, each teacher will get ten time slots.

- You could break it down by grade level, evenly or unevenly (e.g., fifth grade teachers at your school use more advanced technology with their students and therefore need more time for complex projects). You might divide your 240 slots among three grade levels:

EVENLY	UNEVENLY
Grade 3: 80 time slots	**Grade 3:** 70 time slots
Grade 4: 80 time slots	**Grade 4:** 70 time slots
Grade 5: 80 time slots	**Grade 5:** 100 time slots

SCHEDULING *(cont.)*

LAB SIGN UP . . . RESERVING YOUR SPOTS

At the beginning of each six weeks, you can have a sign-up day in the lab. The lab schedule for each week is placed on a clipboard or spread out on a table. Teachers plan computer projects that integrate technology into their classroom curriculum prior to this sign-up day. When they come, they are able to sign up on consecutive days for large projects and then space the rest of their time slots over the six weeks to complete smaller word processing projects or quick lessons.

Some schools organize their system by vouchers. Each open time slot is a voucher. The vouchers (slips of paper that guarantee entrance into the computer lab) are divided among the teachers, and they must take in a voucher each time they visit the computer lab.

In some schools, teachers barter for and trade their vouchers from scheduling period to scheduling period. For example, Mrs. Pittman knows she is doing an intense project this period and may need up to 14 slots; she can trade her vouchers (time slots) with Mrs. Julius, so that this six weeks, Mrs. Pittman has 14 slots and Mrs. Julius has six. For the next scheduling rotation, Mrs. Pittman will have six time slots, and Mrs. Julius will have 14. This allows teachers more flexibility to produce more complex (and even better quality) projects in the lab.

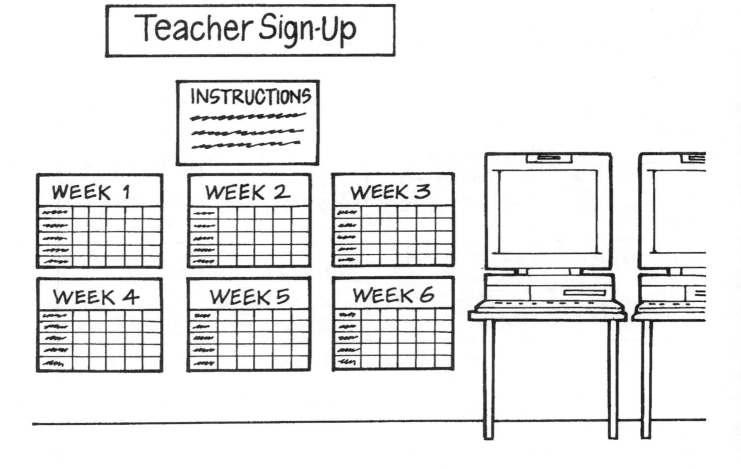

SCHEDULING *(cont.)*

LAB ATTENDANCE

You may want torecord which teachers or grade levels are using the lab with a Lab Attendance Record (page 11). There is a place for each teacher's name, date, and class project. This document will help show how often the lab is being used and what each class is doing in the lab. Because this document will be available to everyone using the lab, teachers will be able to see what is being produced by other classes. A teacher who primarily uses the lab for word processing may see that other teachers are creating number concept slide shows and may have their class try it. See the reproducible attendance record on the next page. A sample attendance record might look like this:

LAB ATTENDANCE RECORD

Please write the date and project in progress each time you use this lab.

Teacher Name	Date/Project	Date/Project	Date/Project

EXAMPLE:

Please write the date and project in progress each time you attend the lab

Teacher Name	Date/Project	Date/Project	Date/Project
Butler	9/4 Publishing Story	9/8 Publishing Story	9/8 Parts of Speech Activity
Jones	9/5 Ancient Egypt Slide Show	9/6 Ancient Egypt Slide Show	9/7 Ancient Egypt Slide Show
Pittman	9/3 HyperCard the Skeletal System	9/4 HyperCard the Skeletal System	9/5 HyperCard the Skeletal System

As teachers sign in their individual classes, they can see what other teachers are doing in the lab and share ideas.

SCHEDULING *(cont.)*

LAB ATTENDANCE RECORDER

Please write the date and project in progress each time you use this lab.

Teacher Name	Date/Project	Date/Project	Date/Project	Date/Project	Date/Project	Date/Project

PLANNING

There are many ready-made technology lessons within this book for those of you just getting started with using technology. As you become more proficient with the use of technology, you may want to create your own technology lessons, based on your students' needs, as well as your own objectives.

Many teachers are overwhelmed at the thought of planning technology lessons for their classrooms, especially if they are inexperienced, unprepared, or untrained. After awhile, you will find that planning technology is as easy as helping students plan any other project from a book report to a science project. Begin where you would normally—the curriculum. What is happening in the classroom? Start with your objectives for the unit or lesson and then think of ways a computer can help your students express what they have learned. Many teachers begin with a software program and ask themselves, "What can my students do with this?" It is much easier to begin with your objectives and your content and ask yourself, "What technology tools can I use to help my students reach these goals?" That way you can be sure that you are using technology to enhance your curriculum and not trying to modify your lessons to fit the available technology.

You may want to use the Technology Lesson Plan Advance Organizer (page 14) to help guide you as you begin. Once you have developed your own style, however, you can change the planning sheet to meet your specific needs. One excellent use of this planning sheet is as a tool for communication. If your school does not yet have a technology coordinator, this advance organizer for teachers can be a great way to share ideas among your staff. Each time a teacher uses the planning sheet to create a lesson for his/her students, he/she can make a copy of the lesson plan to be housed in a notebook in the library or computer lab. Be sure to make copies of the assessment model you used or any advance organizers needed by the students. If all teachers create lesson plans, this notebook can be a wonderful resource. If you are ever stumped for an idea, go to see what other teachers have been doing. Organize the notebook by subject level so teachers can find things easily. It may be a little work in the beginning, but it will save work in the end by providing a wealth of ideas for your students.

IDEAS FOR PLANNING

Plan lessons with specialists at your school.

Combine the talents of classroom teachers, media specialists, technology specialists, and other specialists at your school. Plan activities that span the curriculum and reach beyond the confines of your classroom. You will be doing much of your research outside of the classroom, so involve those teachers who will be helping along the way. The media specialist may have a unique way to complete the research for a particular topic and help give you insight to the best way to organize it.

PLANNING *(cont.)*

IDEAS FOR PLANNING *(cont.)*

Make joint plans with the teachers on your grade level.

For example, set aside one morning a month to brainstorm ideas for integrating technology into your grade level's curriculum. Share what you have done and what you would like to do with your students. You would be amazed to find that many teachers share the same concerns. It is much easier to find solutions together than for everyone to struggle alone.

Plan across the different grade levels.

If you have several people at your school who are interested in technology, form a committee to create a database of good technology ideas for use at your school. Many ideas in this book can be used for more than one grade level. Also, you have many different levels within each grade. Maybe your fourth graders can benefit from technology ideas used at the fifth grade level. Sometimes teachers avoid this because they are afraid of their students repeating the same projects year after year, when actually this process can eliminate that problem altogether. For example, if you take the Story Mapping Lesson Plan on pages 56–57, you can design it differently for each grade level. Third grade students can follow the lesson plan and create a story map for a book they read in class. Fourth grade students can follow the same lesson plan but bring in the element of historical fiction. Teachers can require accurate historical details to appear in a slide show with special focus on the setting being true to the times. Fifth grade students can create story maps from stories they have written—perhaps autobiographies or fantasy stories. They can follow a study of animation, and fifth grade story map slide shows can all contain some form of simple animation. It is amazing how you can take a technology lesson and mold it to fit different grade levels.

Plan with teachers from other schools.

Use the resources available in your district. Find other teachers who are excited about technology and share ideas. You can even have your students become Internet pen pals.

PLANNING *(cont.)*

TECHNOLOGY LESSON PLAN ADVANCE ORGANIZER

Teacher: _____

Topic: _____

Subject: _____

Program(s): _____

Assessment:

_____ Rubric for teacher evaluation

_____ Rubric for peer evaluation

_____ Checklist

_____ Anecdotal

_____ Other

Teacher Objectives and Focus Points:

(These are the skills that you are targeting with this project. Examples: research skills, organization skills, facts, artwork, graphics, writing, creativity, etc.)

   1.

   2.

   3.

Major Content Covered in the *Project* (not the entire unit):

(Examples: If it is a project on the Civil War, you might include any one or more of the following: battles, generals, uniforms, important women, important minorities, causes and effects, major turning points, etc. For a human body project, you might include the following major bones with facts included and interesting facts about the skeletal system.)

   1.

   2.

   3.

Project Requirements: (other things you would like to include, such as maps, sounds, or scanned pictures)

MANAGEMENT

As the computer lab becomes a more integral part of elementary education, it will become a hub of student and staff activity. Teachers needing instructional and technical assistance need to know they can find it in the computer lab. However, you do not have to be a computer expert to provide this help; you only need to have the desire. As a professional maintaining a computer lab, many things may fall under your jurisdiction—from software installation or minor technical problems to joint planning of technology lessons and, finally, staff development.

Here are some useful management ideas to help keep your computer lab running smoothly throughout the year. (If you do not have a computer lab at your elementary school, you may wish to use some of these ideas in your media center or teacher resource room.)

COMPUTER LAB SETUP (See page 16.)

If you wish to make your computer lab truly a technology lab, do not think of it as just a place to use a computer. It should be a center of student productivity. Include stations for video capture and editing, telecommunicating, publishing, and more.

If possible, for behavior management purposes, arrange the computers around the perimeter of the room. This allows the person facilitating the activity to do a quick scan of who is on task.

Student Stations

- Provide your students with computer clipboards (the clips that hold your notes comfortably on the side of your computer). Student projects require notes, research, planning sheets—all kinds of information for students to reference while working. This helps students keep their personal areas organized while helping them get their work done. (For right-handed students these should be mounted on the left side of the computer monitor; for left-handed students they should be mounted on the right. Most manufacturers offer a Velcro attachment so the clipboard can be switched, if necessary.)

- Do not forget about left-handed students. Show them how to switch the mouse to the left side of the keyboard (if possible on your hardware). Another option is to set up a couple of permanent stations for left-handed students. Quite often, left-handed students will not complain about the difficulty of using a mouse with their right hands, but try to make it easy for them by making a few minor adjustments.

MANAGEMENT *(cont.)*

COMPUTER LAB SETUP

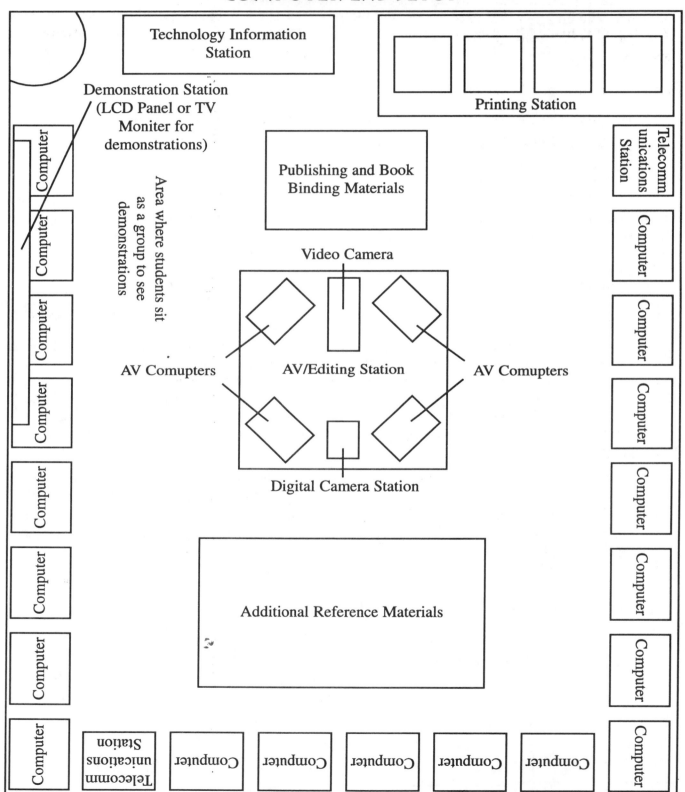

MANAGEMENT *(cont.)*

INFORMATION STATION

Throughout the day, teachers may need assistance ranging from questions about software to computer problems. Set up a help area near the entrance door to your lab to minimize lab interruption. Here they can sign up for lab times, get lesson plan ideas, request assistance, and answer their own software questions.

Contents of Information Station:

- Teacher Update Board
- Technology Lesson Plan Books
- Software Manuals
- Software Help Binder
- Lab Schedule

- Lab Attendance Record
- Computer Maintenance Request Clipboard
- Software Inventory Forms
- Software License Binder

TEACHER UPDATE BOARD

If you do not have an electronic mail system for your staff, it can be very difficult to keep teachers up-to-date with new information and announcements related to technology. Hang a white board or a bulletin board at the information station to keep teachers informed about happenings in the computer lab. Here you can inform teachers of upcoming staff development opportunities in your school or outside of your school, technology conferences, deadlines for student projects, upcoming computer club or technology committee meetings, student software orders, and other important announcements.

MANAGEMENT *(cont.)*

CLIPBOARDS

- **Schedule Clipboard:** Keep your computer lab schedule for each six weeks available for teachers at your information station. Teachers can double check their times and projects and also see if there are open slots when their students are running behind on a project.

- **Computer Maintenance Request Clipboard:** Here teachers can inform the technology specialist, or person in charge, of computer problems. Maybe they need software installed or a printer is malfunctioning. In that case, you may be able to fix the problem before or after school. If it is a more serious problem, you can contact the necessary county or district technicians to help solve the problem.

- **Software Inventory Clipboard:** It is nice to have this available to all so they can be sure they have the proper licensed software loaded on their computers. It is also a good idea to have more than one person responsible for software. For example, if the third grade teachers use some of their instructional budget to purchase software, they need access to the inventory sheets, as well.

BINDERS

- **Technology Lesson Plan Binder:** This is a great way to organize teaching ideas for a technology lab. Whether one person is responsible for these ideas or the whole school contributes activities, it is a fantastic way to offer integration ideas to teachers looking for ways to enrich their classroom learning. It is recommended that you organize these by subject area (language arts, math, social studies, etc.). This will allow third grade teachers to find good lessons from sixth grade teachers and then modify them to fit their own curriculum and skill level needs. Encourage your teachers to add to the Technology Lesson Plan Binder each time they have a new idea. Your school resources will continue to grow and change as technology education changes.

- **Software Help Binder:** Teachers always need quick and easy software tips. Because the day is so full, no one has time to weed through a software manual to have one simple question answered. However, when the lab manager has other responsibilities, he/she may not always be available to answer questions. Make up cheat sheets or FAQ (frequently asked questions) sheets for teachers' quick reference. It is an excellent idea if you are in charge of staff development for your teachers. Each time you do a staff development activity with your teachers or teach them a new skill, put the handouts you create in the binder. Now, teachers will always have access to that information.

- **Software Licensing Binder:** This will help keep track of software licensing. Use your Software Inventory Clipboard to keep track of what is currently loaded. You also need to keep up with the actual licenses for single-user packages, network licenses, lab packs, and site licenses.

- **Lab Information Binder:** What an important resource for a lab! This is a crucial component of an organized lab. However, you may want to keep it out of the reach of students. Based on your situation, these categories may or may not apply. There may be others that need to be included for your technology lab. This is just a suggested outline.

MANAGEMENT *(cont.)*

BINDERS (cont.)

1. Scheduling Information (how scheduling is done in the lab, time slots available, down/maintenance time, etc.)

2. Lab Software (what titles are available on which computers, station information, etc.)

3. Lab Hardware (information about computers, printers, scanners, etc.) This is a very important category. It can help you keep track of what systems need upgrades and how they were purchased (local money, county money, PTA, donations, etc.).

4. County Software (If your county or district makes county-purchased software available to you for review for possible purchase, keep track of what is new.)

5. System Information (important network information—how computers on the network are named, backup information, passwords, etc.) **Note:** Many people are hesitant to record passwords or to make them available to others. In some situations, as schoolwide technology infrastructures grow, there are so many different passwords, it can be difficult to keep track of all of them. What if the person responsible for the system is unreachable and there is a minor problem? The system information and necessary passwords need to be available.

6. School Technology Plan

7. County/District Technology Plan

-   **Examples File Binder:** Designate a special area, maybe a filing cabinet or a bookcase, to contain exemplary student projects. Sharing successful student projects is an excellent way to promote student interest and set expectations. Arrange a filing system (maybe arranged in the same way the Technology Lesson Plan Binder is organized) so that the teacher directing the activity can quickly access good student examples. Within this file, put a disk box. Purchase some extra disks on which to put examples of student slide shows and *HyperStudio* stacks for any type of project that is not printed. Each time you see a great project, save it onto one of these disks. Then, when introducing a new activity, you have a variety of student work from which to choose. It makes it much easier for students to visualize the outcome and, quite often, will raise student expectations.

MANAGEMENT *(cont.)*

BEHAVIOR HINTS

Quite often teachers find that students are on their very best behavior in the computer lab. Even those students who are often bouncing off the walls are so enthralled by technology that they actually stay planted for a 40-minute lesson.

However, without explicit expectations, anything can become chaotic. And with expensive equipment around, you do not want things to get out of control.

Allow whispering.

Students can (and will) quite often answer one another's questions if they are allowed to. While a "no tolerance" rule for talking seems to some like a way to keep students productive, it can also have the opposite effect.

Control the noise level.

Allowing students to whisper sounds great in theory, but 30 students can create a lot of noise, even when working diligently on a project. If controlling noise is a priority, keep an egg timer handy. If the noise level climbs above normal, the whisper privilege is revoked for a short period of time. Set the egg timer for three to four minutes (any more results in lots of student questions and not enough teachers to answer them). Students are not allowed to talk until the buzzer sounds. This will bring the noise level back down and also remind students of the importance of being able to communicate with one another.

Look, no hands!

In your classroom, students are sometimes required to raise their hands to ask a question. But in the computer lab, that takes away valuable time on the keyboard when they could be answering their own questions. Many student questions in the computer lab involve how to do something on the computer (e.g., how to delete a word, how to make a picture larger, etc.). If a student's hand is in the air, not only are his/her own problem-solving capabilities taken away, but whatever the student next to him/her is doing becomes interesting, and a chain reaction of off-task behavior is likely to follow.

Bypass that problem by using cups to request attention. Place disposable cups (I recommend Solo cups or a similar plastic cup because they are more durable than paper, yet still inexpensive to replace if necessary) next to each computer. If a student has a question, he/she places the cup on top of the computer monitor to signal the teacher that help is needed. If the student is able to answer his/her own question before the teacher makes his/her way over there, the cup is returned to the side of the computer.

If you are in a team teaching situation with a professional in the computer lab and the classroom teacher attending with his/her class, develop a signal. If a student has a technical or computer question about how to use a particular tool, place the cup upside down on the computer. If it is a content-related question about what was covered in the classroom, a student can signal the classroom teacher with the cup facing up.

MANAGEMENT *(cont.)*

THE MINI-LESSON

If you have ever sat through a computer course where the instructor talked nonstop for what seemed like forever before allowing you to practice all of the neat things he/she was demonstrating, you will support the mini-lesson. There is so much for students to learn about technology that we, as teachers, want to share it all with them. However, as we share tool after tool after neat trick, students begin to tune out. Somewhere there is a happy medium, and it seems to be around five minutes. Start each and every activity with a mini-lesson. When students are learning a new piece of software, we tend to inundate them with all of the things it can do when they can usually learn it pretty quickly on their own.

When students already know a piece of software, teachers tend to say, "Go on and get started," without talking to them at all about the software. Even if you are only showing them a neat trick about how to change a font or make a picture more spectacular, you are giving them one more tool to make their work the best it can be. Take about three to five minutes each day to share or, better yet, let one of them share a valuable idea on the computer.

MANAGEMENT *(cont.)*

MINI-LESSON EXAMPLES:

Mrs. Loeber's class is typing a Civil War newsletter on the computer. It will take about four visits of 40 minutes each to the computer lab to type in the information, add graphics, edit, do the necessary formatting, and print. Instead of taking 20 minutes at the beginning of the first session to overwhelm students with how to type, change font and style, add pictures, edit, etc., she spends about four minutes at the beginning of each session to show them the tools that will help them get that day's objective met.

Day 1 Mini-Lesson (three minutes)

She reminds her students how to create a document and set its margins.

Her students spend the day typing in their information.

Day 2 Mini-Lesson (three to four minutes)

She shows (or reminds) her students how to change the font and size of the letters for headlines. Then she shows them how to change the text justification to center where necessary and justified on the articles.

She goes over anything that her students struggled with on day one.

Day 3 Mini-Lesson (four to five minutes)

She shows her students how to import pictures into their documents, resize them, and wrap text.

She goes over anything that her students struggled with on day two.

Day 4 Mini-Lesson (three to five minutes)

She reminds her students of how to do final editing (use the Student Editing Checklist, if desired). She also shows them spell check functions and how to catch common mistakes.

Students will retain more because they will have had the opportunity to apply what they learned each day.

Keep it short and sweet.

It is difficult to stop yourself after only three to five minutes. The first time Mrs. Loeber tried to do this, she thought she did a great job and that her lesson was quick—it ended up lasting 15 minutes (and, of course, her students only retained half of what they heard). Practice keeping it short. Keep an egg timer handy to stop yourself from becoming too long-winded. There is always tomorrow.

MANAGEMENT (cont.)

RULES

Have specific behavior expectations for students in the computer lab. Because the computer lab is different from the classroom, you may want to set specific guidelines for student behavior. As you introduce these rules, show the students exactly what it looks like if a student is following a rule and discuss examples of what might constitute breaking a rule. Use a role-playing exercise, if necessary, to demonstrate acceptable behavior.

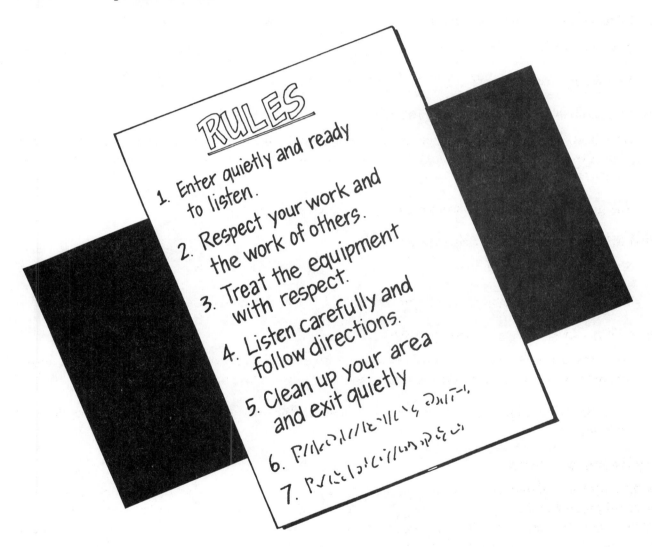

Set up very clear consequences for breaking the rules and be consistent.

Sample Consequences

First offense: warning

Second offense: five minutes off the computer

Third offense: note home to parents and lose remaining computer time

THE ONE-COMPUTER CLASSROOM

Managing a classroom full of 25 or more students is a challenge, even without involving a computer. It is a privilege to have a computer in the classroom, but sometimes you do not feel that way when you constantly hear "Sam got to work on the computer longer than me," or "I never get time on the computer." Part of changing the way you manage the computer in the classroom must come from changing the way you use it. In some classrooms the computer is a place to go when work is completed or a place to play a game. The truth is that we all have unique teaching styles; therefore, we all use technology differently in our classrooms. The secret is to tap into the potential of the computer in the classroom and use it in many ways. Depending on how you use the computer, different scheduling methods will appeal to you. If the computer is used as a free-time activity where students play games, scheduling is not as much of an issue. However, if you are integrating it into your teaching by including technology components in your units, students are responsible for producing technology projects; therefore, they must have larger blocks of equitable time on the computer. Look at the scheduling methods on the following pages and find one that fits your needs.

Traditional Classroom Model

Integrated Classroom Model

SCHEDULING

ASSIGNED TIME

Depending on how you structure your classroom, this may or may not be a viable option. If you have your day structured in small subject blocks (e.g., 40 minutes for math, 50 minutes for language arts, 30 minutes for physical education, 40 minutes for science), each with a whole-group lesson, practice, and a closure activity (or some similar arrangement), this might not work for you. In this type of situation, a student assigned to the computer would be missing a whole-group activity and the work that accompanies it. Also, the time spent on the computer is very limited; the student is not able to make much progress in a five-minute trip to the computer.

However, if you have an integrated schedule with larger, thematic blocks (e.g., 120 minutes for a thematic block, 70 minutes for a Writers' Workshop, 60 minutes for math menus, etc.), assigned time might appeal to you more. (See the sample schedule on pages 26–27.) This method works in an integrated schedule because the large blocks of time usually consist of many different small-group activities taking place in the classroom while you, the teacher, act as a facilitator or "guide on the side." Because each unit/topic being studied in your class contains a technology component, your students know what is required of them during their computer time—work, not play.

When assigning students to a block of time, you can group them in mixed ability groups, and they can choose a name or you can color code them (blue group, yellow group, etc.). For example, if the purple group is on the computer during the math block, the four to five students in the group may work on the computer during that time. During each week or each unit, every group should have computer time during every block. For some units, the technology component may be a group activity so all students in the group are contributing. When you assign an individual activity, students take turns at the computer, based on who is prepared and ready for the technology activity. This method may sound like a scheduling nightmare, but you would be surprised at how easily students are able to adjust once a routine is set.

MIXED ABILITY GROUPS

Blue Group	Yellow Group	Red Group	Purple Group	Green Group
BOB	AUSTIN	DARYL	RENEE	JOHN
DAWN	GEORGE	DIANE	KIMBERLY	JILL
KYLE	MIKE	BILL	JASON	ERIN
BARBARA	BYRON	PAMELA	GARY	DOREEN
MANUEL	JOE	CAROL	JUAN	TERESA

SCHEDULING (*cont.*)

SAMPLE DAILY SCHEDULE

	Monday	Tuesday
Opening Session 8:30–9:00	Monday Map Challenge: Asia (See the Mind Twisters on page 44.)	Tuesday Teaser—calculator decoding
Math Menus 9:00–10:00	Introduce weekly math menus—Do an introductory whole-group lesson on probability; see page 123.	Students work on their math menus; hold a math progress conference with the blue and yellow groups.
Special Area Class 10:00–10:40	Art	Music
Lunch 11:50–12:20		
Silent Reading 12:20–12:50		
Writer's Workshop 10:40–11:50	Open with the status of the class. Tall Tale—continue the writing process for the tall tale. Skills notebook—write compound sentences. The blue group works on the computer.	Open with the status of the class. Tall tale—continue the writing process for the tall tale. Skills notebook—practice placing commas in compound sentences. Do peer editing. The red group works on the computer.
Thematic Unit 12:50–2:20	Continue the flight unit—flight vocabulary review; continue experiments on variables of flight; research flight history; highlight flight in WWII. Technology component—plan a slide show on flight. The green group works on the computer. Flight unit—begin designing and building balsa wood airplanes.	Continue working on flight history research paper. Highlight air safety. Technology component— prepare a slide show on flight. The yellow group works on the computer.
Language Arts/Writer's Workshop 2:20–3:00	Spotlight exaggeration in tall tales. Read *Paul Bunyan* in the anthology, pages 223–225. Find humorous exaggeration phrases. Have teacher-student conferencing. Study spelling.	Locate similes and metaphors in tall tales. Read aloud *John Henry*. Students take notes on similes and metaphors. Hold a writer's workshop on comparative writing. Hold a spelling conference.
Daily Closure 3:00–3:20	*Reminder: The tall tale rough draft must be conferenced by Thursday.	

SCHEDULING *(cont.)*

SAMPLE DAILY SCHEDULE

Wednesday	Thursday	Friday
Students work on math menus. Hold a math progress conference with the red and green groups.	Students work on math menus. Hold a math progress conference with the purple group.	Math menus closure—check on math progress; check up on probability.
Spanish	Technology/Video Production	P.E.
Open with the status of the class. Tall tale—continue the writing process for tall tale. Skills notebook—work on correcting run-on sentences. The yellow group works on the computer. Spotlight revision.	Open with the status of the class tall tale—continue the writing process for tall tale. Skills notebook—work on complex sentences. The green group works on the computer.	Hold a writing conference—tall tale draft—continue writing, share drafts, and engage in peer editing. The purple group works on the computer.
Flight unit—continue airplane design. Continue working on the flight history research paper. Highlight the biological affects of flying. Technology component—prepare a slide show on flight. The yellow group works on the computer.	Flight unit—continue the airplane design. Edit the flight history research paper. Highlight becoming a pilot/flight school. Technology component—prepare a slide show on flight. The purple group works on the computer.	Flight unit—the final copy of the flight research paper is due. Share blueprints for planes. Begin construction. The red group works on the computer.
	**Tomorrow bring, in materials for an airplane model.	

SCHEDULING *(cont.)*

To keep track of whose group is scheduled for computer time during the day, use a paper clip to hang a string from the ceiling over the computer. At each block changeover, hang the coordinating color of construction paper over the technology center. This signals the group that at some point during the small-group activities, they may work on the computer.

Hint: Make one of your daily helpers the technology manager. This person will be in charge of changing the group assignment clip at the computer to alert the group to their computer time.

Sample Schedule:

Block	Monday	Tuesday	Wednesday	Thursday	Friday
Math	Purple	Blue	Red	Yellow	Green
Writer's Workshop	Blue	Red	Yellow	Green	Purple
Thematic Unit	Green	Yellow	Blue	Purple	Red
Language Arts	Yellow	Green	Purple	Red	Blue

EQUITY

Making sure all your students have the opportunity to work on the computer can be very difficult. There are ways to make it easier to manage for you and your students. Choose a visual way to display who has and has not been to the computer. Regardless of how you schedule student time on the computer, this is a successful way to make sure one person is not monopolizing the computer.

The methods on pages 28 and 29 allow you, the teacher, and the students to do a quick scan to see who has had a recent turn on the computer and who still needs the opportunity.

Craft Sticks

Materials: marker, craft stick for every student, two jars/cups

Put each student's name on a popsicle stick. Label one jar "not yet" and one jar "been there." At the beginning of the week or unit, all students start out in the "not yet" jar. Once they have had turns on the computer, they must put their craft sticks in the "been there" jar. This does not mean they cannot use a computer a second time. Whenever the computer is available, it is fair game. However, it does mean that students in the "not yet" jar can bump a student off the computer by taking their craft sticks from the "not yet" jar. You never want your computer to gather dust when it can be productive; however, you do need to allow opportunity for all students.

SCHEDULING *(cont.)*

Clothespins

Materials: poster board (one piece), one clothespin for each student.

Put each student's name on a clothespin. Draw a line down the middle of the poster board. The left side is reserved for students who have not been to the computer; the right side is for those who have been. Once they have had a turn on the computer, they move their clothespins to the other side. Perhaps on this side you could list alternative independent activities once each student has worked on a computer (writer's workshop, reading corner, research, puzzle center, etc.).

SIGN-UP SHEET

You may want to use some blocks of time during your day as priority-based computer time. To use this time, students must sign up to work on a particular project and justify why they need the computer time. For example, if a student's project crashes or if a student is absent, that student may need extra computer time, as compared to a student who just wants to add some snazzy animation or play a problem-solving game for fun. You can decide the order and the amount of time that each student will have to work on a computer. This block of time could be first thing in the morning, during silent reading time, or some other consistent block of time during the day. Keep a sign-up sheet for each week on a clipboard near the technology center. There is a sign-up sheet on page 30, or make your own.

CLASSROOM MEETING

Hold a class meeting to get scheduling suggestions from your students. Share some different scheduling possibilities with them and ask them to share their thoughts and ideas. You will be amazed at some of the wonderful ideas students have to offer. Also, the majority of students often find it easier to follow rules and schedules that they have had a part in creating.

You may find that none of these methods alone will solve all of your scheduling problems. Try a combination of these methods. Maybe you can create your own scheduling variation. Because your classroom is unique, your scheduling needs are, as well. Just do not let your computer sit idle.

SCHEDULING *(cont.)*

COMPUTER SIGN-UP SHEET

WEEK OF _____

Students: Be sure to fill in your name, project, reason you need to work on it, and the time needed to finish it. If any of these columns are left blank, your request will not be considered. Leave the Scheduled Time column blank so you can be assigned a time.

Student Name	Project	Reason	Time Needed	Scheduled Time

PLANNING

Planning for the one-computer classroom requires a different mind set from that for a whole-group situation. Instead of being used with a whole-class activity, generally the classroom computer is used by an individual or a small group. Although you can use many of the same activities, you need to structure the activities somewhat differently.

SUGGESTIONS FOR USING THE LESSON PLANS IN THIS BOOK

These lesson plan ideas are meant to be applicable in a variety of situations—the lab, the mini-lab, and even with a single classroom computer. However, you may find that with only one computer, you will need to restructure some parts of each lesson plan differently than if you have a classroom full of computers. Because many of the activities in this book require planning in advance, your students will be ready to go to the computer at different times. Try using the scheduling methods recommended in the preceding section and the management recommendations below to make each activity work for you.

---

1. When time is limited yet the project is well suited to your unit, allow your students to work in small groups or pairs to complete their projects. Make sure one student is not monopolizing the computer time by using a "keyboard" egg timer. (For example, two students are working together. The egg timer is set for five minutes, and one of the students has control of the keyboard for the first five minutes. When the first five minutes is up, the keyboard responsibility goes to the second student and the timer is reset.) At the end of the project, have each student write a paragraph, telling how they each have contributed to the overall success of their project.

2. Introduce the activity to the entire class. Explain the objectives of the lesson and your expectations. Develop a time line for your unit and allow your students to work on the project individually. Be sure you have project directions clearly posted at the computer work station and a Software Hints Sheet for the specific program being used. This allows each student to work independently without interrupting you during other small-group activities.

3. Occasionally, students will need extra help on the computer. Designate a technology team for your classroom. This can be per project, per software package, or per semester. The technology team should be a list of students who are accessible to any student having problems on a computer. Train these students how to answer questions, how to demonstrate or explain the answer to the student, and how not to solve the problem for the student.

4. Keep up with student progress by using a Status of the Class Management Sheet (page 33). This helps track who is using their time wisely and who may be struggling with the activity.

5. Have student-teacher technology conferences. Allow students to have one-on-one time with you to show you their projects. This allows you to keep close track of progress and achievement.

PLANNING *(cont.)*

INTEGRATING INSTRUCTIONAL SOFTWARE INTO THE CLASSROOM

Instructional software has its own unique niche in the one-computer classroom. Many teachers are familiar with instructional games, but do not see their value. When integrated correctly into the curriculum, instructional software can offer a valuable extension to classroom learning or critical practice for those who need it.

Some instructional software can provide experiences and feedback to students during individual practice time that no worksheet or math page can do. This can be especially valuable for the student who needs the extra reinforcement.

Search for software that offers a variety of experiences and activities, from drill and practice to simulation and on to synthesis. For example, when searching for math software, find a program that questions students in different ways, not just asking them to fill in the blanks. Also, many software packages are too level specific. Check to make sure the activities reach students at a variety of levels.

There are some simulation software packages available that do an excellent job of making history, math, language arts, etc., more meaningful for your students. Excellent examples of this are *MECC's* Trail packages. The *Oregon Trail, Amazon Trail,* and *Yukon Trail* put students in historically and geographically accurate situations and quite often get them emotionally involved. Students begin to value the decisions they make, whether they are solving a math problem integrated into the package or making critical decisions about which direction to travel.

These types of packages often require less planning and management than productivity activities that you do in your classroom. However, there are a lot of misleading educational software packages on the market. Beware of the games that offer lots of bells and whistles but no substance. Choose your software carefully—it can end up being a big waste of money.

Hint: Most educational software dealers and companies will allow you to preview a piece of software before you buy it. It is well worth the effort.

PLANNING *(cont.)*

STATUS OF THE CLASS MANAGEMENT SHEET

Project: _____   **Project Dates:** _____

Student Name													

MANAGEMENT

One of the most important parts of technology management in your classroom is setting behavioral expectations. Many teachers feel they do not know as much about the computer as their students, so they do not give them a clear introduction to it and their expectations regarding its usage. Although many computer novices have a fear of harming the computer, many students have the opposite approach. They are almost hardened to the presence of technology due to their experiences with video games, computers, and other expensive equipment around the home and, therefore, do not treat the machines carefully. It is never too late to teach students how to treat a computer with respect and to reinforce that in your classroom.

At the beginning of the year as you give students a tour of their new classroom, introduce your computer. Set up rules as a class about what you can and cannot do to the computer. If possible, come up with a short set of expectations about computer usage as a class and post them at the computer. If your students are responsible for coming up with the rules, they tend to take ownership of them and their enforcement.

Some Example Rules

1. Be kind to the equipment.
2. Eating and drinking should be done away from the computer.
3. Respect the work of others.

Even where teachers have very open classrooms, mistreatment of classroom equipment should not be tolerated and should result immediately in loss of computer time. The lives of computers are very often shortened by the way they are treated, and they spend time gathering dust in the back of the room because they are not working correctly. You can avoid this by educating your students from the beginning and giving them the responsibility to care properly for their classroom computers.

MANAGEMENT *(cont.)*

AN INTRODUCTION TO HARDWARE

If you have been trained in how to take the computer apart, show your students what the inside looks like. (Students should not try this at home.) Show them the power source and compare it to a light bulb that becomes hotter the longer it is on. This is a good time to explain why food and drink are not permitted around a computer. It is also a good time to talk about the cooling system of a computer (the fan and vents). Explain to them how the vents need to be exposed to allow air to flow in order to keep the computer cool. Show them the delicate workings of the disk drive. Explain why nothing except a computer disk should ever go into the disk drive. In fact, if your students do not use disks, you may want to keep it covered with a piece of construction paper. It can be ruined due to the dust and chalk in the air if not properly cared for. (Try not to do anything permanent to your computer. You never know when it might be passed on to another teacher.)

Explain to your students how they should care for floppy disks. (1) You should never pull the protective covering away from a disk and then try to touch the disk itself. By touching the actual disk, you could damage the disk and all of the work you put on it. (2) Before you take your disk anywhere, make sure it is inside the disk envelope. (3) Never place your disk near a magnet; it will instantly erase whatever is on it forever.

If you have a CD-ROM player, show your students how to change the compact disks (CDs). Students in grades three to five should be able to handle this task, but if you see them mistreating the CDs, designate a few responsible students in your classroom to handle this responsibility.

Discuss the treatment of the cords, keyboard, and mouse. Set expectations about what to do if they become disconnected. Upper grade teachers can train a small group of students about the setup of a computer; primary and middle grades may want to handle this situation themselves or inform their technology specialist. However, you may find some students, no matter what their grade level, know a great deal about computer maintenance.

It is very important to teach students the proper way to treat a computer and inform them that no mistreatment of the classroom computer will be tolerated. You do not have to make students afraid of the computer to do this; just make them aware. Once the mystery of the computer has been taken away, your students will have more respect for the computer and help the classroom community obey the rules.

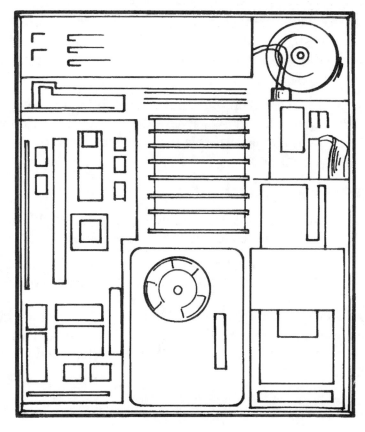

MANAGEMENT *(cont.)*

YOUR CLASSROOM COMPUTER: A TECHNOLOGY CENTER

Your classroom computer should not be just a machine in the corner but a center of productivity. Do not treat the computer as a piece of furniture but put some real thought into its role in your classroom environment.

Technology Center Placement

- If at all possible, try to face the computer monitor towards a wall. This will reduce the distraction the computer causes for other students in your class.

- Try to avoid placing your classroom computer next to a chalkboard or a pencil sharpener. Both of these create dust that can damage the computer's disk drive.

- Try to locate your computer in a place where it can be used as a demonstration station. There will be situations when you will want to use your computer for group demonstrations. Placement near an overhead (if you have an LCD panel [liquid crystal display panel]) or television (if you have an LTV card or an AV machine) can be very helpful for use with the whole classroom.

Technology Center Materials

- Some schools have become so technology infused that computer disks are as much a part of the student supply list as pencils and paper. Have your students bring in computer disks to use throughout the year for special projects. You can usually buy disks very cheaply if you buy them in bulk. Have your students bring in money (a fraction of the cost of buying them separately), use part of your instructional budget, or team up with other interested teachers to order disks from a supply catalog at a discounted bulk rate.

- Purchase a clip attachment for your computer to provide students a place to clip their rough drafts or multimedia planning sheets. These can be purchased for under $10 at most computer or office supply stores.

- If you have a printer (dot matrix), offer a variety of types of ribbons. Use a black ribbon for printing text only and save those fancy color ribbons for printing things with pizzazz. There are even ribbons available that make iron-ons for T-shirts. Have colored paper available for special printing projects.

Technology Center References

- Keep the Software Shortcuts, pages 152–167, available for your students. It will help them become more independent on the computer.

- Make manuals and computer trade books available to your students. You might be surprised at their ability to use them to answer their own questions; besides they are great technical reading.

Assign a student daily or weekly to be the technology manager. This student can help keep the computer area neat, check to make sure the computer is on or off and working properly, alert you to any problems, change the group assignment clip, and do anything else necessary to help you maintain the technology center.

THE MULTI-COMPUTER CLASSROOM

Having multiple computers in your classroom gives you more opportunities to truly integrate technology into your teaching. The multi-computer classroom is usually considered when you have three or more computers (scheduling, planning, and management for the two-computer classroom is probably more similar to the one-computer classroom). Having several computers in your classroom allows you to engage small groups of students (up to the entire class) in technology activities. It also allows you to use the computer in many different ways simultaneously, (e.g., as a math center, as a writing tool, in a science experiment, etc.).

SCHEDULING

Scheduling time for students to work on the computer will always be an issue. There are many methods suggested for the one-computer classroom that will also work in the multi-computer classroom. However, differences do exist.

Scheduling your day in long, thematic blocks (pages 26–27) is probably the best way to utilize the computers in a mini-lab setting. It allows you to have students working on technology all day so the computers never sit idle. However, you still need to arrange your students and activities carefully to best use your time.

ASSIGNED TIME

Assign your students to a computer. If you have five computers in your classroom and 25 students, a group of five students would be assigned to each computer. These students create their projects on this computer, publish writing here, and engage in instructional activities. This makes management somewhat easier because you are only scheduling five students per computer instead of 25. Make each student group as much of a mixture as possible; combine students with different abilities (academic and social), genders, and technology competency levels in each group. Your students will be able to learn from one another and use the strengths and individual talents that they bring to the group. Switch your groups every 6–12 weeks to give your students the opportunity to work with everyone in the class.

PLANNING

The lessons in this book work well in the multi-computer classroom. The main issue is scheduling the time for your students to do their work. When creating your own technology projects, try to create projects that lend themselves to cooperative group activities. For example, create a project (or modify a lesson in this book) so that it has specific jobs. Each day, your students are assigned the jobs they will perform during that day's cooperative technology experience. Have your students use the Job Performance Record (page 40) to keep track of their contributions to the group.

THE MULTI-COMPUTER CLASSROOM *(cont.)*

MANAGEMENT

In any elementary classroom, you will have certain behavioral expectations. Your expectations will not be any different in a multi-computer classroom than in a classroom with one computer. For student management suggestions, refer to the section on the one-computer classroom (pages 34–36).

Use Cooperative Learning Groups

Organize your students into cooperative learning groups so they can get the most out of computer time. Keep in mind, this is different from putting students in a group and telling them to share their work. Effective cooperative learning requires prior planning and adequate management by you, the teacher. It also takes effort and self-control on the part of the students. There are available to teachers many resources that give the whats, hows, and whys of cooperative learning. Refer to these to help make cooperative learning work for you. (For example, TCM 651, 654, 657, and 660: Cooperative Learning Activities for Language Arts, Social Studies, Math, and Science)

Example of Cooperative Learning and Technology

The Inventors and Inventions project (See pages 129–133.)

Students are assigned the following jobs which change from day to day.

Day Two

(On day one, your students worked as a group to select their inventor and made a plan to complete the project.)

Researcher: This person is responsible for finding information and helpful resources to aid in the research of the inventor. This may include using a computer to research via the Internet or CD-ROMs, or it may include going to the school media center to find resources. The student takes notes on the Inventor Research Sheet (page 131). On this day, the student is required to find information about the inventor's early life.

Researcher

THE MULTI-COMPUTER CLASSROOM *(cont.)*

MANAGEMENT *(cont.)*

Graphics Manager: This student searches for helpful pictures, diagrams, artwork, and even animations or video clips for the project. This may include scanning pictures, using the Internet to download graphics, or finding helpful pictures via CD-ROM. This person can also work with the researcher to find good resources.

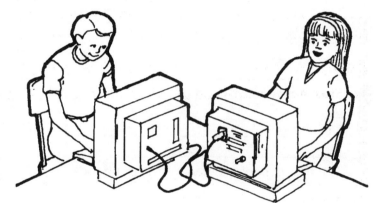

Graphics Manager

Computer Engineers: This pair of students shares the responsibility of working on the actual *HyperStudio* stack (setting up or working on the frame of the stack, adding effects, typing in information). To balance time evenly between the two computer engineers, use an egg timer to measure keyboard time. (Every five minutes have your students switch.) The student who is "off" the computer acts as an encourager and organizer for the student using the keyboard.

Computer Engineers

Hints for Using Cooperative Learning with Technology

Do not expect students to be able to work well in cooperative groups if they have not done so before. It takes very good organization and management, as well as practice. Do not give up on it if your first experience does not go smoothly. Learn from your mistakes, make changes, talk to your students, and give it a second chance.

Use checklists and rubrics to keep students accountable for their share of the work. One of the main challenges with cooperative learning is training students to do their portion of the work and putting in place the checks and balances that will keep students on track. Use a popular cooperative learning checklist or the Job Performance Record on page 40 to manage your students' participation.

Allow for Individual Projects

Cooperative learning helps to keep students involved at all times on projects, but not all projects lend themselves to cooperative group organization. Allow your students to do their own individual projects where they are the only ones accountable. This gives them the opportunity to test their own technology skills and evaluate their own proficiency rather than that of a group's.

THE MULTI-COMPUTER CLASSROOM *(cont.)*

Name: _____

Project: _____

Job Performance Record

Keep track of the duties you perform in your group each day you work on your project. Have the other students in your group initial each day to verify that you fulfilled your responsibilities.

Day # _____
Date: _____
Job: _____
The things I contributed to my group today were:

_____

_____

_____

Student Initials: _____

Day # _____
Date: _____
Job: _____
The things I contributed to my group today were:

_____

_____

_____

Student Initials: _____

Day # _____
Date: _____
Job: _____
The things I contributed to my group today were:

_____

_____

_____

Student Initials: _____

Day # _____
Date: _____
Job: _____
The things I contributed to my group today were:

_____

_____

Student Initials: _____

ASSESSMENT: MAKING IT WORK WITH TECHNOLOGY

Now that you are ready to start integrating technology into your classroom, how do you assess student achievement? Creating multimedia projects and other technology related activities requires a variety of skills. The way we assess students in all areas is changing, and technology projects are an excellent place to start using alternative assessments. Students are no longer evaluated solely by paper-and-pencil tests where there is one correct answer. Students are now required to use their diverse abilities and skills to construct their own responses.

Definition of Assessment:

Assessment is the collection of data or gathering of information regarding one's progress.

PERFORMANCE-BASED ASSESSMENTS

There are all types of assessments that work well with technology. You can evaluate student performance with a checklist, a rubric, or even an anecdotal record. These types of assessments not only give the student information about how he/she did on a particular project but also provide him/her with specific information about the areas that require the most improvement.

Many teachers are finding that with technology projects, you need to look closely at the process, not just the product. A technology project may be the culmination of an entire unit, encompassing over a month's worth of student work and many different types of skills. How do you evaluate that kind of effort from students?

To devise the assessment of a project, it is much easier if you break a project down into manageable parts. These should match the educational objectives of the project.

Think about what you want to evaluate.

Examples for a Kid Pix slide show:

Prior Planning: Did the student complete the planning sheet required?

Use of Technology Tools: Was the student able to use the hardware and software effectively?

Student Research (the content): Did the student provide the required content for the project?

Creativity or Imagination: Did the student take any creative risks?

Grammar/Technical Skills: Did the student meet the requirements for grammar?

ASSESSING STUDENT PRODUCTS

SHARE THE PLAN

When creating a student project, up-front initial student involvement is the key to students taking ownership of the project. When you are getting ready to start a new unit, tell them about the technology component. Allow them to start thinking about it before the content of the unit is even introduced. It will encourage students to be accountable for the content necessary to complete the project.

DISCUSS YOUR GOALS

After introductory lessons in the unit, talk to your students about what they think should be included in the project. What should be required? What should be evaluated?

SHARE THE ASSESSMENT

Put the assessment in terms they understand. Use their words. Try to stay away from teacher jargon; if you used it, your students may not know whether they have met the objective or not. Let them help you determine exactly what is required. If they know this from the beginning, they will be more likely to meet your expectations.

There are sample assessments scattered throughout this book. Because every classroom is different, the assessment that is most effective is the one you create with your students. Use the sample assessments as guides to creating rubrics and checklists that are individualized for your classroom.

SELF-ASSESSMENT

Help your students learn how to use self-assessments as tools to improve their work. Elementary school students very often struggle with organization. Using a self-assessment to help them evaluate their performance on a project as they do it can assist them in achieving the quality they desire.

ASSESSING STUDENT PRODUCTS *(cont.)*

ASSESSMENT EXAMPLE: EXPLORERS

As the explorer unit begins, you, the teacher, give your students the plan for the unit.

Teacher: "Through literature and research over the next six weeks, we are going to discover why and how people explored. What motivated them to go out into the unknown? We will take a look at how they contributed to our society today through their discoveries. You will also have an individual project. Each student will research an explorer and create his/her own multimedia project, using either a *Kid Pix 2* Slide Show or a *HyperStudio* stack about their chosen explorer. We will talk more about the project later. Now, let us learn about explorers."

After your students begin to learn about explorers, you, the teacher, can talk to them about their projects more in depth.

Teacher: "Okay, now that we have learned a little bit about explorers, let us recap what we have already learned and think about what we need to include in a project about an explorer. Any suggestions?"

Student: "How about when they lived and when they explored?"

Student: "How about what they were looking for?"

In the discussion that ensues, you and your students together can decide exactly what might be included in the project. It is important at this point that you guide your students toward the educational goals they have in mind for the project. List the requirements for the project on a piece of chart paper for all of your students to see. You can keep this posted throughout the unit to keep your students on track. Now begin discussing how to assess the project.

Teacher: "Let us talk about how we are going to tell if you are successful on this project. First we need to look at what we have decided as a class to include in the project. What must each project have to be considered as meeting these goals?"

Student: "We need to tell about our explorer and when he lived. That is important. If that is not included, then the project is not complete."

Teacher: "Okay, our first evaluation criteria is to introduce our explorer and tell about when he lived."

Discuss with your students all of the necessary components to the project and exactly what will be evaluated. Decide up front if grammar and spelling will be assessed. Decide if artwork or creativity is important. Ask your students what they think should be emphasized. Come up with a list of things from your students to evaluate. Tell your students what you think is important to do in this project.

ASSESSING STUDENT PRODUCTS *(cont.)*

As a teacher, create a rubric or checklist including the criteria that you and your class have decided upon. The next day, share it with your class.

MULTIMEDIA PRESENTATION 5-POINT RUBRIC

	5	4	3	2	1	0
Overall Presentation	The project flows well, keeps the attention of the audience, and is very interesting.	Project flows well and is interesting.	Majority of project flows well and has some interesting items included.	Majority of project is disjointed and interest level is sporadic.	Project does not flow at all, is poorly presented, and has no interest whatsoever.	No response.
Text Information	The information used is accurate, well written, complete with proper grammar and punctuation.	Majority of the text is accurate, uses proper grammar and punctuation, and mostly flows well.	Uses an acceptable amount of text. Information is accurate. Acceptable grammar and punctuation.	Text information is short and inaccurate. Grammar and punctuation are mostly incorrect.	Information is missing, and grammar and punctuation is misused.	No response.
Graphics and Scanned Images	Images are used to enhance the information and support text. Placement of images is pleasing to the eye.	Images are used to enhance the information and support text. Placement of images is appropriate.	Images enhance the information somewhat. Placement of images is acceptable.	Images used have relevance to information. Not enough images used.	No graphics or scanned images used.	No response.

Teacher: "Yesterday we discussed what we were looking for in this upcoming social studies project. This is the assessment that I put together based on what we as a class decided was important."

Share the assessment.

Teacher: "Will this tool tell us if we did what we set out to do?"

Discuss any changes that may need to be made.

Teacher: "As we work on our projects over the next three weeks, doing the research and putting together our projects, refer to this assessment to stay on track. This is how your projects will be assessed."

This gives your students a choice, and it also gives them information that will guide them as they prepare for the project.

ASSESSING STUDENT PRODUCTS *(cont.)*

SELF-ASSESSMENT

Evaluate your performance on this project, using the following scale:

Not Yet = I did not meet the requirements.

Almost There = I was very close but fell short of meeting the requirements.

I Did It! = I met the requirements.

Above and Beyond = I went above and beyond what was required by doing something extra.

Explain why you earned that rating. Include evidence or reasons that demonstrate it.

1. I selected an appropriate topic.

   Not Yet   Almost There   I Did It!   Above and Beyond

   Why?_____

2. I did the required research or preparation.

   Not Yet   Almost There   I Did It!   Above and Beyond

   Why?_____

3. I was well prepared when it was time to work on the computer.

   Not Yet   Almost There   I Did It!   Above and Beyond

   Why?_____

4. My project has the required parts.

   Not Yet   Almost There   I Did It!   Above and Beyond

   Why?_____

5. I used creativity in my project.

   Not Yet   Almost There   I Did It!   Above and Beyond

   Why?_____

The best thing about my project is _____

I could improve my project if I _____

Things I learned doing this project were

I filled out this evaluation honestly.   Yes ❏   No ❏

Signature _____
Date _____

ELECTRONIC PORTFOLIOS

One of the greatest ways that technology can help us meet our educational goals is by helping us improve the way we assess student progress across the curriculum. Portfolios are already an excellent way to show what a student has achieved; they are not a single piece of information like a test score but a collection of representative student work samples gathered over time. Portfolios also allow the individuality of a student to appear throughout the different types of work included. If a student has a particular gift for writing and self-expression, or art perhaps, it can be much more evident in a portfolio than in a student performance on a test or worksheet.

Portfolios are a collection of student work showing where the student started, the progress the student has made, and a sense of what the student is capable of doing. Portfolios are the overwhelming choice of elementary school teachers because by selecting appropriate work samples to include, they show much more of what the student can do compared to a paper-and-pencil assessment. Portfolios can include things such as the following:

My Goals for the Year

A Favorite Piece of Writing

The Hardest Math Problem I Can Solve

My Neatest Work

The Most Challenging Project I Have Completed

Advantages of Electronic Portfolios over Traditional Assessment

- They provide you with examples of representational student work.
- They provide more information about the students' capabilities than a number or letter.
- They allow students to have more choices about their assessments, thereby causing them to be more motivated.
- They show changes and growth of student achievement over time.
- They encompass a wide variety of skills.
- They are an excellent communication tool for students to share their progress.
- They allow for student individuality.
- They help students develop skills in self-assessment.

Advantages of Electronic Portfolios over Traditional Portfolios

- Electronic portfolios do not take up as much classroom space (boxes, file cabinets full of student work, or sample projects). This makes it easy to add to the portfolio from year to year without its becoming too large and cumbersome.
- Working in electronic portfolios makes it easy to organize and manipulate.
- Electronic portfolios make it easy to scroll through the student samples to find pieces that are significant to the viewer.
- Electronic portfolios make it easy to include large projects (pictures and descriptions), video clips (performances and interviews), and recordings (readings, reflections, and songs). They offer a variety of media for self-expression.

ELECTRONIC PORTFOLIOS *(cont.)*

CREATING PORTFOLIOS

There are software packages designed specifically to help you set up portfolios. Scholastic's *Electronic Portfolio* is an example of one of those packages. It comes with examples at every grade level, a template, and an excellent tutorial that leads you through the process of creating your first portfolio. (Scholastic, (800) 325-6149)

Many teachers think that to create electronic portfolios for (or with) their students, they must purchase an extra piece of software with the one purpose of creating student portfolios. The good news is that there is popular software (possibly already on your computer) that can be used to do the same thing. Many teachers have created wonderful student portfolios with *Kid Pix* and *HyperStudio*. There are also many teachers who have charged their students with the creations of their own portfolios, using these very programs. This reduces your work load and gives your students more freedom, responsibility, and control over their own portfolios.

The Bare Minimum:

> a computer
>
> *Kid Pix 2* or *HyperStudio*

The Basics:

> a computer
>
> *Kid Pix 2* or *HyperStudio*
>
> scanner

The Ultimate Electronic Portfolio Station:

> video camera
>
> multimedia computer w/video editing capabilities (e.g., AV Mac)
>
> digital camera
>
> color scanner
>
> *Electronic Portfolio* (Scholastic), *HyperStudio*, or *Kid Pix 2*

STUDENT-CREATED PORTFOLIOS

Objective: To engage each student in a project to show how he/she has progressed from the beginning to the end of the school year.

Materials: *Kid Pix 2* or *HyperStudio,* a digital camera (optional), a scanner (optional), a folder or shoe box in which to organize work, and a plan

Before you begin the year, plan what you want your portfolio to do and what components you need to include for it to do this. Revisit what is important in student achievement. Look at the process of helping students become better thinkers and helping them recognize their own achievements and decide what you want to be included in the student portfolio.

ELECTRONIC PORTFOLIOS *(cont.)*

KID PIX PORTFOLIO

Recommended for grades two to five:

Students collect samples of their work in the categories of your choice. These are organized in a file folder or shoe box. (If the projects are scanned and put on disk, the project itself can be sent home.)

Throughout the year each student creates slides to go in his/her Portfolio Slide Show. These slides contain information about experiences they have had in the classroom and their personal goals. They can also create slides in reaction to a unit or their performance on a test or project. It is important to keep up with this portion of the project by having students create slides every four to six weeks. This will help show your student's progress from the first day to the last day of the school year.

At the end of the year each student creates a slide show containing the slides he/she created throughout the year, as well as new slides that explain his/her reactions to and feelings about his/her portfolio and why he/she selected the work he/she did. Digital pictures and scanned-in work can be included in the slide show, or you or a parent viewing the portfolio can have the work samples handy as you view each student's slide show.

Organizational tip:

At the end of each unit, have your students create slides about their learning experiences. Have one day a month to create "reflection" slides where each student reflects over his/her progress for that month.

HYPERSTUDIO PORTFOLIO

Recommended for grades three to five:

HyperStudio is an excellent piece of software to use in portfolio creation. *HyperStudio* allows you to easily import text and pictures, include sound, and make additions and changes easily. *HyperStudio* also makes it easy to include video clips and Quick Time movies.

Give your students guidelines about the components of their portfolios. Use a menu at the beginning to allow parents or teachers to navigate through goals, work samples, anecdotal notes, and student projects. Give your students some creative freedom but try to manage the important ingredients of the portfolio.

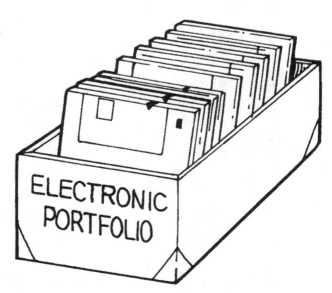

Try to have the portfolio completed (or at least ready to view) by the time you hold your final parent-teacher conferences. Invite each student to share his/her portfolio with his/her parents and to explain what he/she learned throughout the process.

YOU BE THE EDITOR

Help your students learn and practice valuable editing skills without having to spend precious (and limited) computer time typing.

Grade Level: four to five

Duration: 35–45 minutes on the computer

Materials: teacher-generated document, Student Editing Checklist (page 52)

Procedure:

This activity introduces students to editing on computer-generated documents while taking a look at some common editing mistakes. The Student Editing Checklist helps students keep a running tab of which editing duties they have performed. It is a great checklist to use when they are checking their own handwritten work as well.

Before the Computer:

- Students should already have an understanding of the editing process. Do peer editing and individual editing activities with their writing in the classroom prior to this activity.

- Depending on the writing skills that you have covered, you may want to extend the writing attributes they are looking for.

- Devise your own student editing checklist to help keep their editing in tune with what is happening in the classroom.

- To complete the activity, your teacher must first type in a piece of text. (It is recommended that the teacher type in the text in advance so students do not spend the whole time typing with no time left for editing practice. This also allows the teacher to control and vary the type of mistakes the students encounter so that when they find them in their own writing, they will know how to handle them.)

Sample Text:

Once apon a tyme, their was a butiful, but very un fortunate girl She was stuck in the back roome fo a cassle doing the durty werk of her mean stepsisters. Even worse, this young gerl had a cruel step muther who constantly gave her mor things too do

> Regular spelling mistakes (apon, tyme)
>
> Word usage mistakes (too)
>
> Punctuation error (too do)

If possible, choose a familiar story with some humor to make it an interesting story to edit and also for extension activity purposes.

When you save your document with mistakes, you want to protect it so that students will not be able to save the corrections over your document. If he/she did, the unedited version would not be available for others to correct. By protecting your document, you keep it safe for all others to work on.

YOU BE THE EDITOR *(cont.)*

There are several ways to protect a document.

Macintosh Computer:

When working in any program on the Macintosh, you are able to protect a document once it has been created. In order to do this, you need to first create your document. Make sure it is exactly the way you want it. When you quit the software application you are using, go back to the finder and click on your document. Then select Get Info from the File menu. At the bottom of the dialog box, you will see two choices: Locked and Stationery Pad.

Locked: Click on locked. An "x" will appear in the box. When you open your document, you will receive a message that says, "This document is locked so you will not be able to save changes. Do you want to open it anyway?" To save the document, you must give it a new name. A good feature of a locked document is that it cannot be trashed. If you put it into the trash, when the trash is emptied you will be informed that there is a locked document in the trash that cannot be emptied and it will empty the rest of the trash.

(To unlock the document so that you can make changes again, click on your document, select Get Info from the File menu, and click locked again. The "x" will disappear, unlocking your document.)

Stationery: This opens the document as "untitled," leaving the original untouched, just like tearing off a piece of paper; when you use one piece, the rest is unaffected. It can be saved under another name.

YOU BE THE EDITOR *(cont.)*

Any Computer:

When working in an advanced word processing program such as *ClarisWorks, Microsoft Works, Microsoft Word,* etc., you are able to save a document specifically as stationery. Each program works a little differently, but they all offer you the choice between saving it as a normal document or stationery document in the Save dialog box. Create your document as you normally would and then go to Save As. Here you must specify that it is meant to be a stationery document. In some programs these are called templates. If you are not sure if your program offers this option, check the manual's index under stationery or templates.

On the Computer:

Before your students begin editing independently, edit a selection on the computer as a class. Make sure that the selection has all types of errors (i.e., spelling, punctuation, capitalization, etc.). Quite often, a student will think that if they have used the spell check function on the computer, their document is edited. It is important to show them the many kinds of mistakes that the spell check misses. Words can be spelled correctly but used incorrectly. For example, "The young prince looked into here eyes," will show no spelling mistakes. However, the word "here" is not used correctly in the sentence. Some students rely too heavily on spell check to catch all of their errors.

Another easy mistake might be that when the spell check function finds the word "fo" (a very common mistype of the word "of"), it will recommend the word "for." Explain to your students that they should read the word and check each occurrence before replacing it. Show your students how to carefully read in order to find errors. Show them how to temporarily change to a larger font and increase line spacing to make the document easier to read. Also, share the strategy of "bottom to top" reading. When students begin reading their documents at the bottom and read each line until they reach the top, they are forced to look carefully at each word instead of skimming.

Independently, students can open a stationery document that was created by you and correct grammar, punctuation, and spelling mistakes. If possible, provide the number of mistakes in the exercise. This will help them stay on track. After they finish, your students can print their corrected versions of the story.

Options:
- Select a story from a topic you are currently studying, enter it into a computer, and have your students edit it.
- Instead of using a teacher-created document, have your students open a document they have already typed into a computer and edit their own writing as part of this activity.
- If students are having problems with the editing process, create a series of documents with only one type of error in each, for example, a document that has only spelling mistakes, one with capitalization errors, one with missing punctuation, etc. This will allow your students to focus on one type of error and practice identifying it in the computer.

YOU BE THE EDITOR *(cont.)*

Document: _____

Student Name:_____

Date: _____

STUDENT EDITING CHECKLIST

Be sure to carefully check your document with this checklist. Do not rely on the computer to find all of your mistakes.

Meaning and Sentence Structure

_____ I read the document for meaning.

_____ I checked the document for clear and complete sentences.

Spelling and Word Usage

_____ I checked the spelling, using the spell-check tool on the computer.

_____ I read the document carefully for correct word usage (e.g., to, too, two, your, you are, here, hear, etc.)

Capitalization

_____ All sentences start with a capital letter.

_____ Proper nouns that name a specific person, place, or thing have been capitalized.

_____ The title has capital letters where needed.

Punctuation

_____ Each sentence ends with punctuation.

_____ Commas are used in a series of three or more things (e.g., ice cream, pizza, and soda).

_____ Commas connect compound sentences.

_____ Quotation marks are used to show speech (make sure you begin and end them).

_____ I reread the document carefully for all errors.

IMPROVE YOUR WRITING WITH THE THESAURUS

Help your students improve their word usage with the thesaurus function of a word processing program.

Grade Level: four to five

Duration: 40–50 minutes on the computer

Materials: piece of student writing, a word processing program with a built-in thesaurus or a word processing program and a thesaurus program

Procedure:

Before the Computer:

- This activity is especially relevant when you are working on descriptive writing in the classroom. Students are looking for descriptive words but quite often tend to overuse certain words that are familiar to them that they know are descriptive.

- Students need to have an understanding of the thesaurus as a writing reference before this activity.

- Explain that the thesaurus is a book of synonyms that will help them find just the right word. Do some examples before they begin.

Examples:

"The sounds in the empty house scared the children."

empty = vacant, bare, barren, void

scared = terrified, alarmed, dismayed, horrified, panicked, unnerved, startled, spooked

Explain to them that some words will change the meanings of their sentences, so they must be careful about which words they choose.

"The sounds in the bare house dismayed the children."

"The sounds in the vacant house spooked the children."

The meanings of those two sentences are very different. Students need to be sure their replacement words are in tune with the meaning of the sentence.

In class, have your students write descriptive paragraphs. Peer edit them if possible.

On the Computer:

- Have your students type their descriptive paragraphs into a word processing program with a thesaurus. At this point they need to carefully edit their writing for spelling, punctuation, and sentence structure.

- Once their writing is entered, they need to copy and paste it. To copy in most programs consists of selecting your paragraph by clicking and dragging the cursor from the beginning of the paragraph to the end and then selecting Copy from the Edit menu. Students paste a second copy of their writing below the first. Now they have two copies of their paragraph on the same page.

- Students then use the thesaurus to make changes on the second copy of their writing, leaving their original writing untouched. It is worthwhile to have a copy of the paragraph before and after this thesaurus exercise so they can see the effects of the thesaurus on their writing and so they can be sure the meaning stays the same.

IMPROVE YOUR WRITING WITH THE THESAURUS *(cont.)*

To Use the Thesaurus in Various Word Procesisng Programs:

The Writing Center—Double click on the word you wish to change. Select Thesaurus from the Reference menu. You will see a list of synonyms for your selected word. If you see a word you wish to use, click on it. *The Writing Center* will instantly replace your word with the new one. (If Thesaurus appears gray on your computer, you do not have the thesaurus loaded. Check with your technology specialist or whoever is in charge of the software and see if your school purchased the thesaurus portion of the program. If not, it is available from The Learning Company.)

Claris Works—Double click on the word you wish to change. Select Writing Tools from the Edit menu and then choose Thesaurus (or use the Keyboard Shortcut, holding down Command-Shift-Z). It will give you a list of synonyms for your word. Find the word you like, select that word, and then Replace.

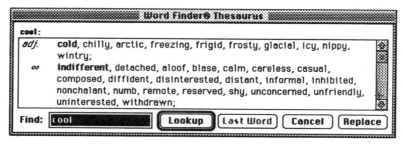

Microsoft Works—Double click on the word you wish to change. Select Writing Tools from the Edit menu and then choose Thesaurus (or use the Keyboard Shortcut holding down Command-Shift-H). It will give you a list of synonyms for your word. Find the word you like, select that word, and then Replace.

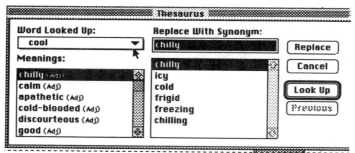

When your students have completed this exercise, let them print a copy to share with their classmates. This activity can help increase vocabulary while improving writing skills.

As students become more familiar with the thesaurus, encourage them to use it on longer selections and to enhance all of their writing with it.

Options:

If your computer time is limited and your students cannot input their own writing, the first time you do this activity structure it like the preceding editing activity. Type in a selection that you have created using very common words (overused/trite words). Then, let your students copy and paste your paragraph. Have them improve the second copy with the thesaurus and then print their document containing the two paragraphs.

PARTS OF SPEECH

Draw attention to the parts of speech in your students' writings.

Grade Level: three to five

Duration: 20–50 minutes on the computer

Materials: word processing document, student directions

Procedure:

Before the Computer:

- This activity is excellent practice once you have covered the parts of speech in class. Be sure to review all relevant parts of speech carefully before assigning this activity.
- The purpose of this activity is to allow your students to recognize the different parts of speech in their own writing.
- It is recommended for students to use a piece of their own writing because it makes the activity more meaningful.

On the Computer:

- Students open a word processing document they created at another time. This could be a newspaper article they typed last semester or a fantasy story from last week. Their task is to find the parts of speech you have covered in their own writing and use a different text style to mark them in special ways. If your students do not have a word processing document of their own, you may type in a story or any type of document for them to access via the network or disk.
- In each word processing program this will be achieved in a different way. When using a popular children's word processing program such as *The Writing Center,* merely double-click on the word to select it and then go to text and select the style you require. In *ClarisWorks,* you select the desired word and select Bold or Outline from the Style menu.

Student Directions:

- Search for the parts of speech in your writing. It is easiest to begin with one part of speech such as nouns and find all the nouns in the document. Then do the same thing with verbs, adjectives, and the rest.
- To change the text style of your word, select the word by double clicking on it (if it is two words together, you must click and drag to select them). Go to the Text menu and select the text style you need.

Nouns—Bold	**Verbs**—Shadow
Adjectives—Underline	**Adverbs**—Italic
Prepositions—Outline	

Options:

- Use a story that was written by your class as a group. This way they will already be familiar with the story when they are ready to begin.
- To reinforce identifying a specific part of speech your class has been focusing on, modify the directions so your students are selecting and changing only one part of speech.

STORY MAPPING

Create your own multimedia library for your classroom by having your students create presentations using pictures, sounds, and special effects. They can create a wonderful product for your classroom while using language arts skills (and others) to create a living book.

Grade Level: two to five

Duration: 60–120 minutes on the computer

Materials: book/story, Story Map Outline (page 58), Story Mapping Storyboard (page 59), Class Slide Show Status Checklist (page 60) optional, Story Mapping Slide Show Assessment (page 61) optional, *HyperStudio* or *Kid Pix 2*

Procedure:

Before the Computer:

- Provide copies of the Story Map Outline for all students.

- Provide copies front and back of the Story Mapping Storyboard for all students.

- Have your students read a story. This can be a story from the class anthology or a story read for independent reading. You can also use a story read aloud to your class. As your students read (or hear) the story or novel, have them complete the Story Map Outline.

- After your students have completed the outline, have them use it as a guide to plan their slide shows. Share the Tips for Creating a Slide Show (page 157) before your students start planning. Also, discuss the assessment model to be used so your students can prepare adequately.

- Have your students complete their slide show planning before they begin working on the computer so they can make best use of their computer time.

The following breakdown of slides is recommended: (This is only a guide; feel free to design a guide as a class or based on your students. You can also give them freedom to plan their own.)

Slide 1:

The title slide tells the name of the story, author of the book, and who is creating the slide show. This should also be decorated for interest.

Slide 2+:

This slide should introduce the characters. It would be appropriate to include a drawing of all or some of the characters here. Your students can use multiple slides to introduce several characters. Suggestion: For those students who cannot draw people, suggest that they draw part of the character (the back part of the character doing something representative of his/her personality), or write a simile of the character—Julie is a young girl who is as sweet as . . ..

Slide 3+:

Have your students introduce the setting. It would be appropriate to draw the main setting or include several slides if there are multiple settings.

Slide 4+:

Introduce and illustrate the main problem/conflict in the story. This may take several slides.

STORY MAPPING *(cont.)*

Slide 5+:

Explain how the problem is solved. Include a picture. Use as many slides as you need.

Slide 6+:

Conclusion. "The End" slide. Be creative!

(How would your main character or another character in the story say goodbye?)

On the Computer:

Your students will need three to six visits to put together their slide shows (recommend finishing two slides per day if possible). Student Management Tip . . . With so many students working on individual slide shows, it is very difficult to keep up with who is nearing completion and who still has lots of work to do. Use the Class Slide Show Status Checklist to keep up with student progress.

Early Finishers:

Encourage your students to try to include animation.

Challenged Learners:

Have your students first retell the story orally while someone records their thoughts. This can be used as a guide to create their storyboards.

Options:

Use stories written by your students.

These slide shows make excellent book reports. It is also a nice project to share with parents in the lab or at conference time.

Assessment Recommendation

Use the Story Mapping Slide Show Assessment as a peer evaluation tool or for teacher assessment.

STORY MAPPING *(cont.)*

STORY MAP OUTLINE

Name: _____

Title: _____   Author: _____

Directions: As you read your story, take notes in the appropriate boxes. You will use this sheet to help you plan your slide show.

Story Setting	Main Characters
Problem	**Solution**

STORY MAPPING *(cont.)*

STORY MAPPING STORYBOARD

Name: _____   Project: _____

Slide # _____

Words/Narration:_____

_____

_____

_____

_____

_____

Slide # _____

Words/Narration:_____

_____

_____

_____

_____

_____

Slide # _____

Words/Narration:_____

_____

_____

_____

_____

_____

Slide # _____

Words/Narration:_____

_____

_____

_____

_____

_____

STORY MAPPING *(cont.)*

CLASS SLIDE SHOW STATUS CHECKLIST

Fill in your class list. After each trip to the computer lab, students may check off each finished slide.

Student Name	Number of slides in show	Title page								The End	Done

STORY MAPPING *(cont.)*

STORY MAPPING SLIDE SHOW ASSESSMENT

Name: _____

Slide Show Title: _____

Slide show including a title and ending slide.

Not Yet   Almost There   Good Job   Excellent

The slide show clearly described the setting.

Not Yet   Almost There   Good Job   Excellent

Slide show introduced the main characters.

Not Yet   Almost There   Good Job   Excellent

Slide show explained the problem and the solution.

Not Yet   Almost There   Good Job   Excellent

Slide show illustrations showed detail and creativity.

Not Yet   Almost There   Good Job   Excellent

Slide show text followed grammar rules.

Not Yet   Almost There   Good Job   Excellent

I liked _____

I recommend _____

Comments: _____

READ ALL ABOUT IT!

Let parents read all about what is happening weekly in your classroom—without you having to stay up late on Thursday night typing up a newsletter. Get your students involved, teach them about news, and save yourself some time.

Grade Level: three to five

Duration: varies

Materials: Article Organizer (page 64), word processing program such as *The Writing Center*

Procedure:

Before the Computer:

If possible, have someone who works at a local newspaper come talk to your students about what it is like to work for a newspaper.

Group your students into the following positions:

Sports Writers: These students write articles about what is going on in physical education. They can also spotlight students in the class who are involved in sports outside of the classroom (e.g., highlighting Beth's gymnastics meet or Tommy's soccer team).

Lifestyle/Living Writers: These reporters write articles about things that are happening to students and teachers that affect their lives (e.g., a new pet, a new student, a moving experience, a field trip, a trip to grandma's).

Fine Arts: These students cover the latest in art and music classes. Emphasize the importance of the arts in school.

Food/Dining Reporters: Students and parents can send in ideas for delicious, nutritional snacks for this area. These reporters also keep parents up-to-date on the weekly lunch menu and the happenings in the cafeteria.

Classroom Reporters: These students report on things that are happening in the classroom. Topics can range from a science experiment or a poetry publishing to a great technology project.

Editors: The newspaper editors help other students by checking their work for content, checking grammar, helping students select pictures for their articles, and checking the final appearance of the paper. They can also include an occasional editorial.

Student Spotlight: Spotlight a student each week. Talk about the student's family, hobbies, favorite subject in school, etc. (It is a good idea to have an outline to follow for this, so each student will get the same coverage.) It is great for self-esteem, and it also helps parents get to know their student's classmates.

Make up your own categories to include each week, depending on the needs of your parents and the goals of your newspaper staff.

Your student groupings should stay in place at least long enough for your students to become familiar with their positions but not so long that they get bored. The recommended time is about three weeks (three articles). The first time you group them, use your judgment (with what you know about your students' strengths and weaknesses) to place them in a category that suits them. As time goes on, allow them to make their own choices. Try to give your students the experience of working in different areas. You may find that your students find niches that suit their talents and where they work well. Once your students have had a chance to work in each position, give them some freedom to choose their permanent positions.

READ ALL ABOUT IT! *(cont.)*

On the Computer:

Have your students work independently or in groups to enter their articles into the newspaper document. Working together provides students with additional editing support and feedback. Keep examples of good articles handy for your students to refer to as needed.

Schedule

This is a recommended schedule for a paper that would be published and sent home each Friday afternoon. This may not work for you and your class, but use it as a guideline to create a schedule that will work.

Friday afternoon (a week before printing) reporters have a newspaper meeting to decide what will be covered in next week's edition. (This is an excellent time for teacher input and guidance.) Reporters make suggestions for stories they would like to see in the paper, and students vote on their favorites. Article assignments are made. This gives students the weekend to think about their articles and what needs to be done.

Monday–Wednesday: During writer's workshop time, students gather information about their topics, doing research, conducting interviews with school staff, etc. Students work on organizing their information into well-developed articles.

Wednesday afternoon: All students must have their final copy finished and signed by two editors.

Thursday and Friday: Students type their articles into the newspaper document.

Friday afternoon: Editors make the final style changes and editing decisions. All artwork is added and copies are made for each student to take home.

Options:

- Encourage students who are struggling with newspaper writing to work with another student as they develop their notes into an article.

- Print a class newspaper monthly instead of weekly.

READ ALL ABOUT IT! *(cont.)*

ARTICLE ORGANIZER

Use this organizer to help you gather information and organize your article. All questions may not apply.

Topic: _____

_____

Who? _____

_____

What? _____

_____

When? _____

_____

Where? _____

_____

Why? _____

_____

Notes: _____

_____

_____

Do your rough draft on a different page, using the notes above. Write your final copy here. When it has been approved by two editors, you may begin typing it into a computer.

Headline: _____

Article: _____

_____

_____

_____

_____

_____

This article has been carefully proofread for content and grammar.

Editor Signature: _____

Editor Signature: _____

HOW-TO SLIDE SHOWS

Students struggle with technical writing. Create a how-to presentation that helps students see how to give step-by-step instructions.

Grade Level: three to five

Duration: 50–120 minutes on the computer

Materials: topic, notes/research, How-to Planning Sheet (page 66), *Kid Pix 2* or *HyperStudio*

Procedure:

Before the Computer:

- Help your students select their topics. It is crucial to their success that your students choose topics they can describe. Some may choose processes that are too involved and some, too common. Encourage them to choose something that they know how to do well; it will help them explain it.

- Tell your students first to do the process they choose several times. Then, as they do it, take notes on each step.

- Have your students write down all the materials and instructions needed to complete their chosen activity. Then they will be ready to put their instructions into a narrative form on their planning sheets. (Do not limit students to the format on the planning sheet. It is meant to be only a guide. If their creativity takes them in another direction, they can use a piece of paper folded into fourths or sixths as their own planning sheet.)

- They should not rely too heavily on diagrams—instructions should be clear enough that the diagrams are only enhancements.

- Have them share their instructions with an editing buddy. A fellow student can help them find the gaps in their instructions.

On the Computer:

- Have your students use their planning sheets to create a slide show about how to do their chosen activity. They should use sound, pictures, and diagrams.

- This can also be organized as a *HyperStudio* stack. Create a step-by-step explanation of the procedure they are explaining with buttons that make sound, diagrams, and whatever other resources are available.

Once the slide shows are complete, they will make an excellent center. Those students who choose things such as folding a napkin into a sailboat, making a pinwheel, or paper folding/cutting exercises can provide meaningful activities for your classroom. Bring in the necessary materials, and students can go to the computer to try to follow the directions.

Have your students fill out a response to the activity. What would have made the activity easier to perform? What would you have done differently?

Options:

- If a student is struggling to identify all of the steps, have a second student perform the activity while the struggling student takes notes on each step.

- Do this activity as an introduction or follow-up to how-to speeches or a technical writing unit.

HOW-TO SLIDE SHOWS (cont.)

Student Name:_____ Teacher: _____

HOW-TO PLANNING SHEET

If you need more slides to complete your instructions, use the back of the page.

1. Title and Introduction

2. Materials

3. Step 1

4. Step 2

5. Step 3

6. Conclusion/Finished Product

BIOGRAPHICAL VIGNETTES

Help make the lives of significant people meaningful to your students by creating mini-films about their roles in history.

Grade Level: four to five

Duration: 70–130 minutes on the computer

Materials: Biography Planning Sheet (page 69), Storyboard Planning Sheet (page 70), other research materials, *Kid Pix 2* or *HyperStudio*

Procedure:

Before the Computer:

- When helping your students select significant people to research, you can allow them to choose anyone at all or you can have them choose from a listing of historical people. (See the recommended list on page 68.)

- If your class is studying a topic such as the Civil War, you can have your students choose people who played a part in the Civil War. Other options are available on the next page.

- Using reference materials such as books, periodicals, multimedia encyclopedias, and the Internet, students complete research about the persons they have chosen to study.

- Encourage your students to find sound bytes and interesting pictures whenever possible.

- Once their research is done, they use a Storyboard Planning Sheet or a paper folded into sixths, to plan before going to the computer.

- You may want to come up with a slide show outline as a class or use the recommended order below.

Slide Show

Slide One: Title Slide   **Slide Two:** Introduction   **Slides Three and Four:** Early Life
Slides Five and Six: Adult Life   **Slides Seven and Eight:** Accomplishments
Slide Nine: Slide Show created by_____.   **Slide Ten:** The End

Hyper Studio Stack

Title Card Menu:

Early Life   Adult Life   Accomplishments   Credits

These are only recommendations. If your computer time is limited or the project is too long, mold it to fit your needs.

On the Computer:

- Have your students take their planning sheets to a computer.

- Using a slide show program, your students will create individual slides for a slide show and then put them into a slide show presentation (or *HyperStudio* stack).

- Once your students have become comfortable with a variety of multimedia programs (e.g., *Kid Pix 2, Kids Studio, HyperStudio,* etc.), allow them to select the program that best fits their needs.

Options:

- If your students create *HyperStudio* projects, they can all be linked together with a table of contents page. Create a button for each biography available and link it to that stack. This would be a wonderful resource for your students.

- To condense this into a mini-research project, have your class gather information about one person. Each student creates one slide about the individual. Combine the slides into one show.

BIOGRAPHICAL VIGNETTES (cont.)

FAMOUS MEN IN HISTORY

Richard Allen	Frederick Douglass	Martin Luther King, Jr.
Crispus Attucks	E.B. Dubois	Abraham Lincoln
James Baldwin	Thomas Edison	Jesse Owens
Benjamin Banneker	Benjamin Franklin	Booker T. Washington
James Beckworkth	Joe Hill	George Washington
George Washington Carver	Langston Hughes	Eli Whitney
Christopher Columbus	John Paul Jones	

FAMOUS WOMEN IN HISTORY

Jane Addams	Dorothea Dix	Sacajawea
Susan B. Anthony	Amelia Earhart	Elizabeth Cady Stanton
Clara Barton	Helen Keller	Harriet Beecher Stowe
Mary McLeod Bethune	Florence Nightingale	Harriet Tubman
Elizabeth Blackwell	Rosa Parks	Sojourner Truth
Lucy Burns	Molly Pitcher	Phillis Wheatley
Rachel Carson	Pocahontas	
Shirley Chisholm	Betsy Ross	

OTHER OPTIONS:

People of the Civil War	Presidents	Famous Authors

BIOGRAPHICAL VIGNETTES *(cont.)*

BIOGRAPHY PLANNING SHEET

_____

(Name of Person)

I. Early Life

     A. Birth/Death Dates

     B. Birthplace

     C. Education

     D.

     E.

II. Adult Life

     A. Education

     B. Marriage/Family

     C. Career

     D.

     E.

III. Accomplishments

     A.

     B.

     C.

     D.

     E.

Notes:

_____

_____

_____

_____

BIOGRAPHICAL VIGNETTES *(cont.)*

STORYBOARD PLANNING SHEET

Name: _____   Project: _____

Slide # _____

Words/Narration:_____

_____

_____

_____

_____

_____

Slide # _____

Words/Narration:_____

_____

_____

_____

_____

_____

Slide # _____

Words/Narration:_____

_____

_____

_____

_____

_____

Slide # _____

Words/Narration:_____

_____

_____

_____

_____

_____

BOOK REVIEWS

Add a new twist to book reports—multimedia.

Grade Level: four to five

Duration: 50–140 minutes on the computer

Materials: Book Review Organizer (page 72), *HyperStudio* Planning Sheet (page 73) optional

Procedure:

Before the Computer:

- Have each student choose and read a book that you have approved.

- As your students read, have them take notes of pertinent information in their organizers.

- Students should also begin collecting biographical information about their authors. (The Internet is an excellent resource for information about children's literature and authors.)

The book does not have to be finished for students to begin the planning and construction of their *HyperStudio* stacks.

On the Computer:

- Have your students use their planning sheets to create book reviews in *HyperStudio*. Refer to the Software Shortcuts section of this book (pages 152–167) for *HyperStudio* hints.

- Encourage your students to use all resources available, such as a scanner, digital camera, Quick Time movies, etc.

Options:

- This project can be created from a novel, a literature selection from a class anthology, or even a story read aloud in class.

- Focus on a particular genre. Allow your students to create a book review about a historical fiction book or a fantasy book.

BOOK REVIEWS *(cont.)*

BOOK REVIEW ORGANIZER

Title: _____

Author: _____

Genre: _____

About the Author:

_____
_____
_____
_____

Other Books by This Author:

_____
_____
_____

Book Summary:

_____
_____
_____
_____
_____

Book Review:

Did you enjoy it? Was it what you expected? Would you recommend it to a friend? Why or why not?

_____
_____
_____
_____
_____

Other Books in This Genre:

_____
_____

BOOK REVIEWS *(cont.)*

HYPERSTUDIO PLANNING SHEET

Project: _____

Student Name: _____

Title Card

Buttons/Links: _____

Notes (Text/Sounds/Animations): _____

Card 1

Buttons/Links: _____

Notes (Text/Sounds/Animations): _____

Card 2

Buttons/Links: _____

Notes (Text/Sounds/Animations): _____

Card 3

Buttons/Links: _____

Notes (Text/Sounds/Animations): _____

Card 4

Buttons/Links: _____

Notes (Text/Sounds/Animations): _____

Card 5

Buttons/Links: _____

Notes (Text/Sounds/Animations): _____

ROPIN' THE WIND . . . WRITING TALL TALES

Help your students create entertaining tall tales that come to life on the computer.

Grades: three to five

Duration: 60–120 minutes on the computer

Materials: examples of good tall tales, Tall Tale Planning Sheet (page 75), Storyboard Planning Sheet (page 76)

Literature Link: *American Tall Tales* by Mary Pope Osborne

Procedure:

Before the Computer:

- Read some good tall tales to your students. *American Tall Tales* by Mary Pope Osborne has many good tales to read aloud.

- There is also a good public television Tall Tale/Fairy Tale video series starring well-known personalities that are funny.

- Tall tales are difficult to write, so be sure your students get some good examples before they attempt to write their own. Pick out some characters to discuss.

  — What makes them so interesting?

  — What obstacles did they face (an enemy, a grizzly bear, a tornado, a winter storm)?

  — How did they use their wits or their strength to overcome that obstacle?

Some heros win by their wits and some use brute force, but they almost always prevail in the end.

- Make two copies of the Tall Tales Planning Sheet for each student. Fill the first one out about a tall tale they have read in class or you have read aloud. Once students have a clear understanding of the parts of a tall tale, they are ready to begin planning their own.

- Before working on the computer, each student should also complete a Storyboard Planning Sheet for his/her slide show.

On the Computer:

- Your students can create their slide shows in *Kid Pix 2,* using the planning sheets where they have organized their slides. Remind your students of the characteristics of a good slide show. (See Tips for Creating a Slide Show, page 157.)

- Depending on your students experience with *Kid Pix 2,* and the complexity and detail of each slide, preparation should take about 10–15 minutes per slide.

- When all slides are completed, your students can put them together in a slide show and share them with the class.

Tall Tale Heroes and Heroines:

Davy Crockett—the rugged frontiers man

Sally Ann Thunder Ann Whirlwind—the outrageous fictitious wife of Davy Crockett (She wears a hornets' nest for her Sunday bonnet.)

Paul Bunyan—a logger in the Great Lakes area (His words froze in mid-air and then thawed out and were spoken in the spring.)

Options:

Allow struggling students to choose a popular tall tale hero or heroine and create a slide show about his/her adventures.

ROPIN' THE WIND . . . WRITING TALL TALES *(cont.)*

TALL TALES PLANNING SHEET

Create your own tall tale by using the planning suggestions below. Remember to exaggerate and use humor.

Hero or Heroine (you can include a "sidekick" if you wish)

Appearance:

_____

_____

Characteristics (wit, strength, etc.)

Example: "He/she walked like an ox, ran like a fox, and swam like an eel."

_____

_____

Foe or Force Against Hero (This can be person or force, such as an act of nature.)

Example: "A tornado was so powerful it picked up Hawaii and moved it 600 miles (960 km)."

_____

_____

_____

Beginning: Introduce your hero and the problem he/she faces.

_____

_____

_____

Middle: Tell about the struggle between the hero and the foe. Give humorous details.

_____

_____

_____

End: Share how the hero outsmarts or overpowers the foe.

_____

_____

_____

ROPIN' THE WIND . . . WRITING TALL TALES *(cont.)*

STORYBOARD PLANNING SHEET

Name: _____   Project: _____

Slide # _____

Words/Narration:_____

_____

_____

_____

_____

_____

Slide # _____

Words/Narration:_____

_____

_____

_____

_____

_____

Slide # _____

Words/Narration:_____

_____

_____

_____

_____

Slide # _____

Words/Narration:_____

_____

_____

_____

_____

GEOMETRIC PICTURES

Shapes are all around us. Help your students recognize the presence of geometric shapes everywhere by having them create pictures composed entirely of geometric shapes.

Grade Level: three to five

Duration: 30–60 minutes on the computer

Materials: math journal/activity about shapes

Literature Link: *The Greedy Triangle* by Marilyn Burns

Procedure:

Before the Computer:

- An excellent way to introduce this activity is by reading *The Greedy Triangle* by Marilyn Burns. This book explores the "jobs" of the different shapes in the world around us (e.g., the triangle as a piece of pie, a musical instrument, a sailboat sail, etc.). Sharing this book with your students will open up many possibilities and spur their imaginations to create clever pictures.

- After sharing this book, have your students write in their math journals or on a piece of paper all of the geometric shapes you have discussed during your geometry unit. Encourage them to write down the correct spelling and examples on their paper; it will help avoid lots of questions as your students work independently on a computer.

On the Computer:

- Each student will create (in *Kid Pix 2* or another similar art program) a picture using the geometric shapes, they have learned about in class.

- Every part of the picture must be a geometric shape.

- They must include at least five different shapes and they should all be labeled. (You can require more, less, or a different combination, such as an entire picture out of squares, etc.)

Possible choices:

Space Figures

cone, cylinder, sphere, rectangular prism, cube, pyramid, etc.

Plane Figures

circle, rectangle, triangle, square, pentagon, hexagon, etc.

Suggestions

A city street

A house and a yard

The court or playing field of a favorite sport

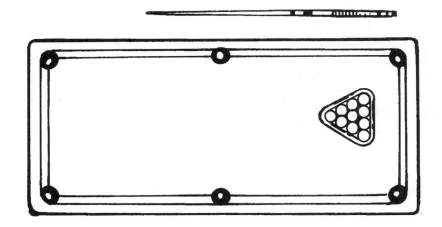

Options:

Assign each student a shape. They must then create a *Kid Pix 2* picture using that shape in as many ways as possible. Put the shapes together into a slide show about geometry. Have your students create introduction slides and slides that tell about each shape.

WHAT'S IN A NUMBER?

Students show multiple representations of a single numeral in this whole-class slide show.

Grade Level: three to five

Duration: 20 minutes on the computer

Materials: math journal or notes

Procedure:

Before the Computer:

- A number can be represented in so many different ways. Use this activity to improve your students' thinking about numbers.

- Present a number to your class. It can be any number, but some recommended numbers are 16, 36, 64, 144 (choose numbers with many different possible representations). These are good numbers because they are square roots and have lots of possibilities.

- It is the students' charge to show the number in a variety of ways. Have students brainstorm about all of the possible ways to represent this number and then record these in their math journals. Each student should be able to engage at his/her own level of mathematics understanding.

Example:

36 is 3 tens and 6 ones.

36 is 30 plus 6.

36 is 36 ones.

36 is 100 take away 64.

36 is 3 dozen.

36 is 6 squared.

36 is 6 times 6.

- Have students pick their favorites. Guide them into picking different ones so that your class slide show will show a wide variety of interpretations.

WHAT'S IN A NUMBER? *(cont.)*

On the Computer:

- Each student creates a *Kid Pix 2* picture about the way he/she represented the class number. Have students record or type explanations (e.g., "36 is . . ."). Have each student save it as (their name36).

- Using all of the entries in your class, make a *Kid Pix 2* Slide Show about the number.

Management Tips:

- If all of your students are working on different computers, they must be compiled onto one disk or one computer to create this slide show.

- If all of your students are saving to the classroom computer, create the slide show on the hard drive.

  If all of your students are saving to the network server, you can access their work from the networked computers and create your slide show on the computer. If you cannot access all slides from the networked computers, copy the slides from the server onto a disk. Compile your slide show on this disk.

- If all of your students are working on separate computers, save the documents onto a disk and then compile them on a single hard drive.

Early Finishers:

Create title slides, introduction slides, and end slides.

Options:

- Assign different numbers to different groups. Have your students create several different picture representations of their numbers. Each group will then create group slide shows about their numbers.

- Print out the pictures created by your students and make a class book. Students can continue to add to the book throughout the year as they learn more advanced operations and concepts.

WHAT'S IN A NUMBER? *(cont.)*

WHAT'S IN THE NUMBER 36?

Students work together to show many different ways to represent the number 36.

PICTOGRAPHING

Take your students through the first step of graphing by creating simple pictographs in *Kid Pix 2*.

Grade Level: three
Duration: 30 minutes on the computer
Materials: survey information, *Kid Pix 2*
Procedure:

Before the Computer:

- Have each student select a topic to survey classmates about. Students record their information on paper. Sample Topics: Student Pets, Favorite Music, Favorite Subject in School
- Encourage your students to give their classmates at least three choices (e.g., Student Pets: dog, cat, bird). It is also a good idea to include an "other" category for those students who do not fit into one of the three categories listed.
- Teach your students how to use a legend. Depending on the number of students surveyed, one *Kid Pix 2* stamp might equal one, two, or five students.

On the Computer:

- Have your students type in the title (topic) of their graph.
- Have them use the straight line tool and the shift key to make a perfectly straight line for their X axis. Have them do the same thing for their Y axis. Label them both accordingly.
- Create a legend. How many students will each stamp represent?
- Put the topics along the X axis.
- Stamp in the correct number of student responses.

Tip: Show your students how the improper spacing of their stamps can distort the graph's information. (For example, if a column of three stamps reaches as high as a column of five stamps, the information might look the same.)

Software Hint:

Your students can create their own stamps in *Kid Pix 2* by clicking on a stamp they do not need to use on the graph and selecting Edit from the Goodies menu. Here they can use the dynamite tool to totally erase the old stamp. Using the pencil, they can create the stamp they need. Remind your students to restore the original so the next student will have access to all of the *Kid Pix 2* stamps.

Options:

Have your students create pictographs about something you are studying in social studies or science.

Examples:

- Who would you vote for in the presidential race?
- state populations
- types of plants around our school

THE CHOCOLATE FACTORY

Students turn candy bars into math problems.

Grade Level: three

Duration: 30–40 minutes on the computer

Materials: math journals, *Kid Pix 2*

Literature Link: *Charlie and the Chocolate Factory* by Roald Dahl

Procedure:

Before the Computer:

- This activity is a wonderful introduction to a unit on multiplication.

- Read a selection from *Charlie and the Chocolate Factory* to get students excited about this activity.

- Your students have just been named marketing directors for a giant chocolate factory. This chocolate factory has a new chocolate bar coming out, and your students must decide how to make it and how it should be packaged.

- Before their times on the computer, your students can make notes in their math journals about their ideas.

  Restrictions:

  - The candy bar must have 12 chocolate squares, each the same size.
  - The candy bar must be symmetrical. No odd shapes. (This is a cost effective measure demanded by the Chocolate Bar Wrapping Department.)

On the Computer:

- Your students must draw a model of each idea they have. They should be encouraged to come up with at least three. Show them how to write the number of squares in number form: 3 x 4 (three squares by four squares). Each candy bar must be clearly labeled.

Back as a whole group in math class:

- Discuss which candy bar is most practical. Why might some sell better than others?

- Make up multiplication problems for each candy bar.

Options:

- Your students can come up with packaging ideas/gimmicks to sell their candy bars.

- Your students can create an advertising jingle.

If this candy bar catches on, students can create another candy bar with 20 squares.

MODEL MULTIPLICATION

Understanding the concepts of multiplication and division is an important step towards mathematics success. With this lesson, your students can demonstrate their understanding by creating a model of a math problem.

Grade Level: three

Materials: math journal or math notes, a multiplication or division problem, *Kid Pix 2*

Procedure:

Before the Computer:

As a math journal activity, have your students solve several multiplication problems and explain them. This works well with a problem-solving activity.

On the Computer:

Students must draw a picture of a multiplication problem. The problem must be stated on the page.

Options:

- Have your students create pictures displaying addition or subtraction problems.
- Have your students write a word problem to fit each picture.

DRAW ME A FRACTION

Your students will demonstrate their understanding of fractions by drawing pictures of fractions as they appear in real life.

Grade Level: three to four

Duration: 30–40 minutes on the computer

Materials: math journal or math notes on fractions, *Kid Pix 2* or other graphic program

Procedure:

Before the Computer:

- As you teach fractions in regular class activities, be sure to point out where fractions occur in real-life situations.

- Have your students take notes on the different types of fractions: fraction of a whole and fraction of a group.

    Fraction of a whole: 1/4 of the pizza is pepperoni, 3/12 of the window is broken

    Fraction of a group: 1/3 of the coins are pennies, 3/10 of the girls wear glasses

On the Computer:

   Have your students create pictures showing fractions in real-life situations. They must show one of each type of fraction (part of a group, part of a whole).

Example:

DIVISION SLIDE SHOW

Long division is a difficult process for fourth and fifth graders to master. Use a multimedia program to make great student-created long division models. This process helps students break down and understand the steps while adding their own creativity.

Grade Level: Fourth

Materials: *Kid Pix 2* or a similar program, a long division problem, *Kid Pix 2* Slide Show Planning Sheet (page 87)

Procedure:

Before the Computer:

- Have each student choose a long division problem to use in a slide show. Examples done in class or in class math books are fine.

- Have each student solve his/her problem on a piece of blank paper. Now the problem must be broken down into steps. It is a good idea for you to do an example for your students and show each step, where it begins and ends.

- Using the *Kid Pix 2* Slide Show Planning Sheet, separately plan each step to demonstrate the process of long division.

- Your students must also plan their explanations (narrations) for each slide on a storyboard. This is very important because it shows that your students know what each step means.

DIVISION SLIDE SHOW *(cont.)*

On the Computer:

Using *Kid Pix 2,* have your students create one slide for each step.

Example:

> **Slide 1:**
>
> Show the problem.
>
> **Slide 2:**
>
> Solve the first part of the problem.
>
> **Slide 3:**
>
> Continue to solve the problem.
>
> **Slides 4–8+:**
>
> Use as many slides as necessary to solve the problem.

It is easiest to use Save As . . .. Create the first slide, save it as slide one. Make the necessary changes to slide one to complete the next step and then Save As . . .. Do slide two, and so on. This helps with continuity and actually makes the division problem seem animated. (Do not forget to create an introduction slide and an ending slide.)

Using Slide Show, your students create a slide show, putting their steps in order.

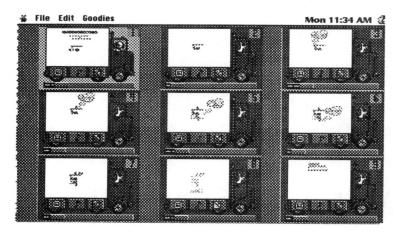

Options:

- Students who are not working on long division should use a simpler problem or another operation (subtraction/borrowing, addition/carrying).

- Students who are really struggling with this process should work with a buddy to get their plans ready for the computer.

- Do not use fancy transitions in between slides they cause a loss of continuity.

- This idea may also be used with multiple digit multiplication, addition, subtraction, and problem solving.

DIVISION SLIDE SHOW *(cont.)*

KID PIX SLIDE SHOW PLANNING SHEET

Title Slide

Buttons/Links: _____

Notes (Text/Sounds/Animations): _____

Slide 1

Buttons/Links: _____

Notes (Text/Sounds/Animations): _____

Slide 2

Buttons/Links: _____

Notes (Text/Sounds/Animations): _____

Slide 3

Buttons/Links: _____

Notes (Text/Sounds/Animations): _____

Slide 4

Buttons/Links: _____

Notes (Text/Sounds/Animations): _____

Slide 5

Buttons/Links: _____

Notes (Text/Sounds/Animations): _____

COOKING WITH MEASUREMENT

Help your students see how measurement plays a part in everyday life, by selecting a favorite recipe to contribute to a class cookbook.

Grade Level: three

Duration: 20–40 minutes on the computer

Materials: My Recipe (page 89) filled in, Cookbook Organizer (page 90), publishing or word processing program such as *EasyBook*

Procedure:

Before the Computer:

- As you learn about measurement, discuss the different types of measurement that we use everyday. Share cooking measurements and cooking tools with your class.
- Explain the abbreviations used for common cooking measurements.
- Ask your students what would happen if they confused teaspoons and tablespoons.
- Have your students bring in their favorite recipes.
- Talk about the measurements found in the recipes. Are there any you did not discuss as a class? (a pinch, a dash)

Just for Fun: To introduce the lesson, try cooking in class. Select a recipe such as chocolate chip cookies or sugar cookies. List all of the ingredients on the board. Ask your students to estimate how much of each ingredient goes into the recipe. Make a batch of cookies and taste them. Then give your students the correct measurements for all ingredients and make the cookies again. Taste test and compare the results. Discuss this process and the role that measurement plays in cooking.

On the Computer:

- This is best organized as a center. Before your students begin, set up the cookbook document in a publishing program such as *EasyBook* (if you do not have a program that makes books, any word processing program will do).
- Have your students take turns at the computer to enter their recipes.

This is a great peer editing exercise.

- As each student has his/her turn at the computer, have him/her edit the preceding recipe for mistakes. It would be a good idea to keep all recipes in a folder next to the computer for the peer editors to refer to if they have questions.

Hint: If you would like to organize your cookbook into sections (appetizers and snacks, main courses, desserts, etc.), have your students bring their recipes in ahead of time. Assign each student a page number and set up your document accordingly.

Options:

- When you are studying a particular region or country, make a regional cookbook.
- Have a tasting day where students bring in samples of their recipes. Encourage parents to let students do all cooking that is not dangerous, especially the measuring.
- Use the Cookbook Organizer to keep track of which students have entered their recipes and which ones have been edited.

COOKING WITH MEASUREMENT *(cont.)*

Name: _____   Parent's Initials: _____

Date: _____   Date Due: _____

MY RECIPE

Copy a favorite family recipe. Make sure you copy all abbreviations very carefully. Have a parent/guardian check over the recipe for mistakes when you are finished.

Preheat oven to: _____   Serves: _____

Ingredients:

_____   _____

_____   _____

_____   _____

_____   _____

_____   _____

_____   _____

_____   _____

_____   _____

Directions:

_____

_____

_____

_____

_____

_____

_____

_____

COOKING WITH MEASUREMENT (cont.)

COOKBOOK ORGANIZER

Student Name	Recipe	(✓) Done	Edited By

GREETINGS FROM . . .

Write home from the city, state, or country that you are studying. Your students can create geographically accurate postcards, using the interesting things they have learned.

Grade Level: three to five

Duration: 30–60 minutes on the computer

Materials: research about a country or place

Procedure:

Before the Computer:

- Have your students research the city, state, or country you are studying in class. For example, in a study of the pyramids, your class can create postcards from Egypt.

- Set up research questions that all your students must answer. This research will help them create their postcards.

    1. What kind of land forms are in our country?

    2. What kind of animals live here?

    3. What types of plants grow in this climate?

    4. What do people do for fun here?

    5. Why do people visit this area?

    6. Are there any interesting cultural events that take place here?

On the Computer:

- Your students will take this information into account as they design the covers of their postcards in a drawing or painting program. Print out the picture.

- Your students must then write the message on the back. The message should describe the kinds of things they can do in the place they are visiting.

Options:

This can also be done as a mini-research project. Instead of doing it in conjunction with a social studies unit, allow each student to pick a place (maybe even out of a hat) he/she would like to visit. Then have students create postcards from different places. It would make a great bulletin board.

A RESEARCH SCAVENGER HUNT

Help your students become comfortable using CD-ROM for research by sending them on an exciting scavenger hunt through a multimedia encyclopedia.

Grade Level: four to five

Duration: 20–30 minutes

Materials: Let's Go on a Scavenger Hunt (page 93), CD-ROM multimedia encyclopedia

Procedure:

Before the Computer:

Demonstrate to your students how to use a CD-ROM encyclopedia. Make sure you show them how to search in a variety of ways; word search, title search, pictures, maps, sounds, etc.

On the Computer:

- This makes an excellent center. This particular scavenger hunt was created using the *New Grolier Multimedia Encyclopedia.*

- Depending on topics and regions you are studying in class, you can make up a scavenger hunt that is more relevant to your curriculum.

Answer Key

1. Alligators have broader snouts than crocodiles and their teeth are hidden, not exposed like they are in crocodiles.

2. Plateau of Tibet

3. Estonia, Lithuania, Belarus, Russia

4. Thomas Kyd wrote *Spanish Tragedy*, the first revenge tragedy in English literature.

5. A goat-like mammal from India

6. Siberian range, Eastern Russia

7. varies with each student

8. varies with each student

Options:

- When your are studying a particular topic, relate all scavenger hunt questions to the topic.

- Students are able to improve their research skills while building a knowledge base for the upcoming unit of study.

A RESEARCH SCAVENGER HUNT *(cont.)*

LET'S GO ON A SCAVENGER HUNT

Use the *Grolier's Multimedia Encyclopedia* to answer the questions below.

1. What are the differences between alligators and crocodiles?

   _____

   _____

   _____

2. In East Asia, what region (plateau) has an elevation of 13,000 feet (3,943 m) or more? (Hint: Use a topographical map to find elevation.)

   _____

3. Name two countries that border the European country of Latvia.

   _____

   _____

4. What is Thomas Kyd famous for?

   _____

   _____

5. What is a tahr?

   _____

   _____

6. Where are the Yablonovy Mountains?

   _____

7. Play musical selections by Bach, Beethoven, Handel, Mozart, and Tchaichovsky. Which is your favorite?

   Title:_____

   _____

   Why? _____

   _____

8. Make up your own scavenger hunt question.

   _____

   _____

MY TOTEM POLE

Your students will learn to appreciate the meaning behind symbolic Native American totem poles as they create totem pole representations of themselves.

Grade Level: two to three

Duration: 30 minutes on the computer

Materials: *Kid Pix 2*, journal activity

Procedure:

Before the Computer:

- During a unit about Native Americans (or another culture that created totem poles), introduce your students to a variety of totem poles. Explain their purpose and the symbolism they represented.

- Instruct them to think about things that represent them. Answer these questions in a journal activity:

  What do you like to do?

  What are you good at?

  What are some of your hobbies?

  Do you have any pets?

  Students think of images that represent them.

On the Computer:

- Students use *Kid Pix 2* to create a symbolic totem pole.

- Next to each picture, have your students explain how that symbol plays a role in their lives.

- Print these, mount them on colored paper, and display them on a bulletin board.

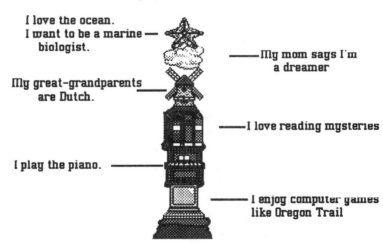

My Totem Pole

I love the ocean.
I want to be a marine —
　　biologist.

My great-grandparents
　　are Dutch.

I play the piano. ————

————— My mom says I'm
　　a dreamer

————— I love reading mysteries

————— I enjoy computer games
　　like Oregon Trail

Options:

Allow your students to "carve," (draw) more authentic totem poles with *Kid Pix 2* drawing tools. Encourage your students to use symbols that were more common in the totem poles of the Natiive Americans.

LAND HO! EXPLORER RESEARCH PROJECT

Help your students gain an appreciation for the discoveries of the great explorers while utilizing research skills, language arts skills, and creativity.

Grade Level: four

Duration: 70–130 minutes on the computer

Materials: Explorer Fact Sheet (page 98), *Kid Pix 2* Slide Show Planning Sheet (page 99), Explorer Slide Show Assessment (page 101) optional

Procedure:

Before the Computer:

- Have each student research the dates of an explorer's life—his early life, the area explored, who he explored for and why, and the importance of his discovery, if any.

- Have your students use the Explorer Fact Sheet to help them organize their information.

On the Computer:

> *Kid Pix* **Slide Show**

- Use a *Kid Pix 2* planning sheet to organize and plan slides.

    Slide One: (Title Slide)

- the explorer's name

- the years of his life (e.g., 1425–1499)

    Slide Two:

    introduction (Explain the purpose of the slide show or project.)

    Slide Three:

    his early life (three facts)

    Slide Four:

    where he explored (Include a map showing his routes.)

    Slide Five:

    the reasons he explored (What was he looking for?)

    Slide Six:

    outcomes of his exploration (What did he find?)

    Slide Seven:

    bibliography

    Slide Eight:

    The End

- Each slide show must contain at least one map showing where the explorer traveled.

LAND HO! EXPLORER RESEARCH PROJECT *(cont.)*

This project also works well with *HyperStudio*.

Have your students use the *HyperStudio* Planning Sheet (page 100) to help them organize their information.

Title Card:

Early Life

Reasons for Exploration

Routes of Exploration (Include a map here.)

Outcomes of Exploration

Bibliography

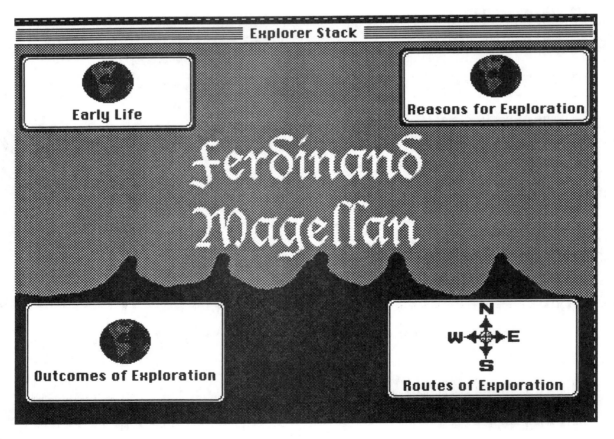

Options:

   Link each student's *HyperStudio* stack together with a table of contents card. This makes it very easy for students and visitors to explore all of the stacks.

LAND HO! EXPLORER RESEARCH PROJECT *(cont.)*

EXPLORERS:

Vasco Nunez de Balboa	Leif Eriksson	Zebulon Pike
John Cabot	Prince Henry the Navigator	Francisco Pizarro
Samuel de Champlain	Henry Hudson	Sacajawea
Christopher Columbus	Juan Ponce de Leon	Sieur de La Salle
Francisco de Coronado	Meriwether Lewis and William Clark	Jedediah Strong Smith
Hernando Cortes	Ferdinand Magellan	Hernando De Soto
Bartolomeu Dias	Jacques Marquette and Louis Joliet	Amerigo Vespucci

LAND HO! EXPLORER RESEARCH PROJECT *(cont.)*

EXPLORER FACT SHEET

_____
(explorer)

_____
(dates of his life)

Birthplace:_____

Early Life Notes: _____

_____

_____

Where did he explore? _____

_____

_____

Why did he make the trip? _____

_____

_____

_____

Outcomes of his exploration: _____

_____

_____

_____

_____

Sources:

_____

_____

_____

_____

LAND HO! EXPLORER RESEARCH PROJECT *(cont.)*

KID PIX SLIDE SHOW PLANNING SHEET

Title Slide

Buttons/Links: _____

Notes (Text/Sounds/Animations): _____

Slide 1

Buttons/Links: _____

Notes (Text/Sounds/Animations): _____

Slide 2

Buttons/Links: _____

Notes (Text/Sounds/Animations): _____

Slide 3

Buttons/Links: _____

Notes (Text/Sounds/Animations): _____

Slide 4

Buttons/Links: _____

Notes (Text/Sounds/Animations): _____

Slide 5

Buttons/Links: _____

Notes (Text/Sounds/Animations): _____

LAND HO! EXPLORER RESEARCH PROJECT *(cont.)*

HYPERSTUDIO PLANNING SHEET

Title Slide

Buttons/Links: _____

Notes (Text/Sounds/Animations): _____

Slide 1

Buttons/Links: _____

Notes (Text/Sounds/Animations): _____

Slide 2

Buttons/Links: _____

Notes (Text/Sounds/Animations): _____

Slide 3

Buttons/Links: _____

Notes (Text/Sounds/Animations): _____

Slide 4

Buttons/Links: _____

Notes (Text/Sounds/Animations): _____

Slide 5

Buttons/Links: _____

Notes (Text/Sounds/Animations): _____

LAND HO! EXPLORERS RESEARCH PROJECT *(cont.)*

EXPLORER SLIDE SHOW ASSESSMENT

Explorer: _____

Group Members: 1. _____

2. _____

3. _____

4. _____

5. _____

Slide show includes facts from research.

Not Yet   Almost There   Good Job   Excellent

Slide show contains illustrations and a map.

Not Yet   Almost There   Good Job   Excellent

Slide show illustrations show detail and creativity.

Not Yet   Almost There   Good Job   Excellent

Slide show text follows grammar rules.

Not Yet   Almost There   Good Job   Excellent

Comments: _____

_____

_____

_____

TRAVEL BROCHURE

Have your students create their own professional looking brochure about a place they have been to or researched. They should integrate research skills, geography, writing, and creativity into this project.

Grade Level: three to five

Duration: 90–180 minutes on the computer

Materials: research about a country or any place that interests you, pictures of the place you researched, Travel Brochure (pages 103–104)

Procedure:

Before the Computer:

- Have your students use encyclopedias, CDs, trade books, and other media to research a country, region, state, or city to create a travel brochure.

- Encourage your students to take notes about their region or country, collect or draw pictures, and find interesting facts during their research.

- Have them enter their research on the Travel Brochure pages before working on a computer.

On the Computer:

- Each student will begin work on a landscape oriented (see File-Page setup) word processing document with two columns.

- When using a regular word processing program (such as *ClarisWorks*, *The Writing Center*, *Microsoft Works*, etc.), it is important to remember the order of the categories on the planning sheet since it will not print out correctly unless you use the suggested order. If using a book publishing program such as *EasyBook*, the program will print out your pages in order without having to create them in order.

Printing Options:

- Have students print out the first pages of their documents and then have them reinsert their documents into the printer to print the second page on the other side.

- Print out both pages separately, mount them on construction paper, and then fold them.

- Pictures and maps can be scanned, copied, or created. Each student should try to include at least one map along with good descriptive writing.

Options:

- — Visit Arizona (or another state).
- — Visit the Grand Canyon (or another landmark).
- — Experience the Northwest (or another region).
- — Come to Greece (or another country).

As a class, you may want to change the components of the travel brochure, based on what you are researching.

TRAVEL BROCHURE *(cont.)*

Student Name: _____

Date: _____

Important Facts

Bibliography

TRAVEL BROCHURE *(cont.)*

What to See

- -

Map Including Points of Interests

ANCIENT CIVILIZATIONS SLIDE SHOW

Studying ancient cultures is such a rewarding experience. Let your students share their findings through multimedia slide shows.

Grade Level: three to five

Duration: 60–120 minutes on the computer

Materials: Ancient Civilization Research Sheet (page 106), Ancient Civilization Planning Sheet (pages 107–108), Project Checklist (page 109)

Procedure:

Before the Computer:

- Have your students work to research their country's focus questions (so that every focus question is answered in every slide show).

- Each of your students will create an independent slide show.

- In the classroom and media center, have your students research the following questions about their ancient civilizations:

    1. How did the ancient civilization meet their basic need for food?
    2. How did the ancient civilization meet their basic need for shelter?
    3. How did the ancient civilization meet their basic need for clothing?
    4. How did the ancient civilization meet their need for transportation?
    5. What forms of art and architecture did the ancient civilization develop?
    6. What forms of recreation did the ancient civilization develop?
    7. What advancements in science did the ancient civilization provide?

- Help your students complete their research by using the Ancient Civilizations Research Sheet.

On the Computer:

When the research is complete, use class time to plan for the slide show. There is a planning sheet available for those students who need structure and organization. You may find that some students create better slide shows when planning on their own.

Options:

- Use the above research questions to study and create projects about other civilizations.

- Expand your studies to compare the ancient times to the present.

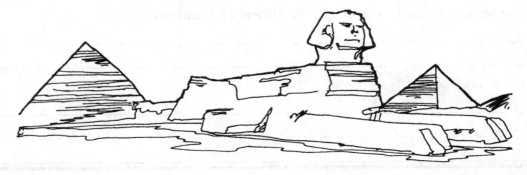

ANCIENT CIVILIZATIONS
SLIDE SHOW *(cont.)*

ANCIENT CIVILIZATION RESEARCH SHEET

Civilization:_____

  1. How did the ancient civilization meet their basic need for food?

    _____

    _____

    _____

  2. How did the ancient civilization meet their basic need for shelter?

    _____

    _____

    _____

  3. How did the ancient civilization meet their basic need for clothing?

    _____

    _____

    _____

  4. How did the ancient civilization meet their need for transportation?

    _____

    _____

    _____

  5. What forms of art and architecture did the ancient civilization develop?

    _____

    _____

    _____

  6. What forms of recreation did the ancient civilization develop?

    _____

    _____

    _____

  7. What advancements in science did the ancient civilization provide?

    _____

    _____

Other Interesting Facts:

_____

_____

ANCIENT CIVILIZATIONS SLIDE SHOW *(cont.)*

Student Name: _____

Civilization: _____

ANCIENT CIVILIZATION PLANNING SHEET

Title Slide _____

Introduction to Slide Show _____

Food _____

Shelter _____

Clothing _____

Transportation _____

ANCIENT CIVILIZATIONS SLIDE SHOW *(cont.)*

Student Name: _____

Civilization: _____

ANCIENT CIVILIZATION PLANNING SHEET *cont.*

Art and Architecture _____

Recreation _____

Advancements in Science _____

Transportation _____

Free Choice _____

The End _____

ANCIENT CIVILIZATIONS SLIDE SHOW *(cont.)*

Student Name:_____

PROJECT CHECKLIST ANCIENT CIVILIZATIONS

Required Contents:

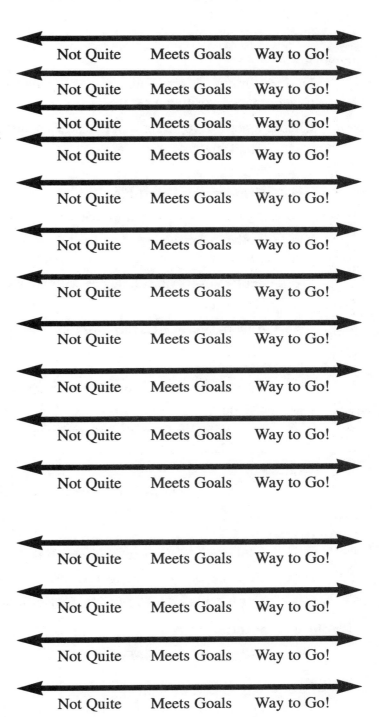

The slide show was well planned.

    Not Quite   Meets Goals   Way to Go!

The slide show contains a title slide.

    Not Quite   Meets Goals   Way to Go!

There is an introduction to the slide show.

    Not Quite   Meets Goals   Way to Go!

The slide show describes the food of the ancient civilization.

    Not Quite   Meets Goals   Way to Go!

The slide show describes the shelter of the ancient civilization.

    Not Quite   Meets Goals   Way to Go!

The slide show describes the clothing of the ancient civilization.

    Not Quite   Meets Goals   Way to Go!

The slide show describes the transportation of the ancient civilization.

    Not Quite   Meets Goals   Way to Go!

The slide show describes the art and architecture of the ancient civilization.

    Not Quite   Meets Goals   Way to Go!

The slide show describes the recreation of the ancient civilization.

    Not Quite   Meets Goals   Way to Go!

The slide show describes the science advancements of the ancient civilization.

    Not Quite   Meets Goals   Way to Go!

The students included at least one other interesting fact.

    Not Quite   Meets Goals   Way to Go!

Extras:

The student included detail and creativity in his/her artwork.

    Not Quite   Meets Goals   Way to Go!

The student scanned in pictures to include in his/her presentation.

    Not Quite   Meets Goals   Way to Go!

A map is included to show the location of the ancient civilization.

    Not Quite   Meets Goals   Way to Go!

A bibliography is included.

    Not Quite   Meets Goals   Way to Go!

ADVERTISING

Your students will discover and learn to appreciate the art of advertising by using advertising strategies to create public service announcements.

Grade Level: five

Duration: 60–120 minutes on the computer

Materials: Public Service Announcement Outline (page 111), *Kid Pix 2* Slide Show Planning Sheet (page 112), *Kid Pix 2*

Procedure:

Before the Computer:

- During a unit on advertising, allow your students to use some of the popular advertising strategies to get across a positive message.

- Choose a popular topic for a public service announcement, for example:
  — Don't Smoke
  — Don't Litter
  — Help Prevent Forest Fires

- This is a good activity to incorporate into a persuasive writing unit.

- Evaluate other advertisements and public service announcements before your students begin planning their own. What makes the good ones so effective? What makes the bad ones fall short?

- Share popular advertising strategies with your students.

  Famous People

  > Advertisements use recognizable, sometimes influential people (or characters) to promote their product.

  Testimonials

  > People who have used the product share how it changed their lives or worked for them.

  Slice of Life

  > Advertisers use average, everyday people that their target audience can relate to, to sell their idea.

  Lifestyle

  > Showing people who live a certain type of lifestyle (wealthy, carefree,etc.) engaging in the desired outcome is often a way advertisers hook their audience.

  Scientific Proof

  > Commercials quote surveys or research to validate their product.

- Have your students select and identify a method to use in their own announcements.

- Use a *Kid Pix 2* Slide Show Planning Sheet to plan your public service announcement.

On the Computer:

Have your students use *Kid Pix 2* Slide Show to create their public service announcements.

Options:

Share them with the class. See if you can identify which advertising strategy has been used.

ADVERTISING *(cont.)*

PUBLIC SERVICE ANNOUNCEMENT OUTLINE

Problem to Correct (What are you trying to change?)

_____
_____
_____
_____
_____

Target Audience (Who do you want to hear your message?)

_____
_____
_____
_____

Advertising Strategy (Which strategy will be most effective for your message?)

_____
_____
_____
_____

Where and when should this ad appear to reach the target audience?

_____
_____
_____
_____

Slide 1:_____

Slide 2:_____

Slide 3:_____

Slide 4:_____

Slide 5:_____

Slide 6:_____

ADVERTISING *(cont.)*

KID PIX 2 SLIDE SHOW PLANNING SHEET

Title Slide

Buttons/Links: _____

Notes (Text/Sounds/Animations): _____

Slide 1

Buttons/Links: _____

Notes (Text/Sounds/Animations): _____

Slide 2

Buttons/Links: _____

Notes (Text/Sounds/Animations): _____

Slide 3

Buttons/Links: _____

Notes (Text/Sounds/Animations): _____

Slide 4

Buttons/Links: _____

Notes (Text/Sounds/Animations): _____

Slide 5

Buttons/Links: _____

Notes (Text/Sounds/Animations): _____

BUILDING A FOOD CHAIN

Help your students understand the connections of a food chain by having them create one of their own.

Grade Level: three

Duration: 30 minutes on the computer

Materials: notes/text about a food chain, including a specific animal

Procedure:

Before the Computer:

- Have each student choose an animal.
- Each student must research the animal he/she has chosen and its part in the food chain before working on the computer.

On the Computer:

Have each student draw a picture of the food chain, using his/her own illustrations, as well as clip art and stamps available from any graphic programs.

Options:

Group your students into categories to see how interrelated the food chain is; for example, look at the food chains of ocean animals or pond life.

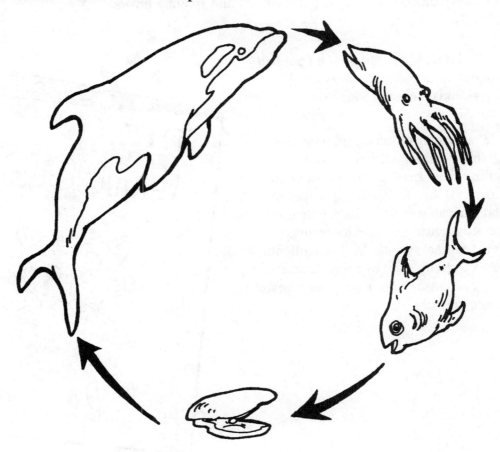

PUBLISH IT!

Make mini-books about animals. Make them easily and colorfully with a program like *EasyBook*.

Grade Level: three to five

Materials: reference materials, Animal Research Sheet (page 115), Mimi-Book Planning Sheets (pages 116–118), *EasyBook* (or another publishing program)

Procedure:

Before the Computer:

- Have each student select an animal to research.

- Decide as a class the information that must be included about all animals or use the research sheet provided.

- Encourage your students to use a variety of resources for their research. Tap into sources such as CD-ROM encyclopedias and the Internet.

On the Computer:

Have your students use their research sheets or their notes to compile their animal books. If your students struggle with composition or if your computer time is very limited, use the Book Planning sheets included. This also allows you to keep up with the amount and relevance of the content being included, as well as grammatical and spelling errors.

Options:

- Instead of a book, your students can publish their research as a *HyperStudio* stack, including sounds and even video of their animals.

- Choose a particular group of animals to research that go along with what you are studying in other areas of your curriculum. For example, if you are studying Australia, your students can research Australian animals; or if you are focusing on environments, endangered animals would be an excellent topic. Pick a group such as ocean animals, predators, or dinosaurs to make your research topics more specific.

PUBLISH IT! *(cont.)*

ANIMAL RESEARCH SHEET

_____
(Name of Animal)

Appearance:
_____
_____
_____

Life Cycle:
_____
_____
_____

Habitat:
_____
_____
_____

Diet:
_____
_____

Interesting Facts:
_____
_____

Resources:

Book/Resource: _____

Author: _____

Publisher:_____

Page #:_____

Book/Resource: _____

Author: _____

Publisher:_____

Page #:_____

PUBLISH IT! *(cont.)*
MINI-BOOK PLANNING SHEETS

Name: _____

Teacher: _____

Animal: _____

Introduction

Appearance

PUBLISH IT! *(cont.)*
MINI-BOOK PLANNING SHEETS

Teacher: _____

Habitat

Animal: _____

Life Cycle

Name: _____

PUBLISH IT! *(cont.)*

MINI-BOOK PLANNING SHEETS

Name: _____

Teacher: _____

Animal: _____

Diet

Interesting Facts

FLOWERING MINDS

Help amateur botanists gain an appreciation for the parts of a flower.

Grade Level: five

Duration: 30 minutes on the computer

Materials: black construction paper (optional), a flower (optional), science vocabulary, science notes/journal

Procedure:

Before the Computer:

- Bring flowers into your class. Give each student (or group of students) a flower and a piece of black construction paper. (optional)

- Help them create cross sectional views of their flowers.

- In a guided discovery activity, your students will dissect their flowers, revealing their parts.

- Discuss the common names and the scientific names. Make sure students have the correct spelling of the scientific names.

   Vocabulary:

   — cross section
   — petal
   — stamen
   — pistil
   — sepal
   — receptacle
   — pedicel

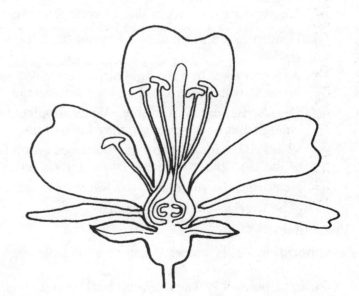

- Encourage your students to take notes in their lab journals about their flowers. Help them record their observations.

On the Computer:

- Each student will draw a picture of his/her flower.
- Label each part and then print it out.

Options:

- Ideally, each student or group of students should have a different type of flower to dissect. On each diagram, the student should list his/her flower's common name and scientific name. Then, when they draw their pictures, your students can see how the concepts they have learned apply to all flowers.

- Bind all examples together into a book. This will be a wonderful classroom resource.

THE WATER CYCLE

Your students will demonstrate a knowledge of the water cycle and its individual steps in a meaningful way. This activity is an excellent assessment of your students' understanding of the water cycle.

Grade Level: four to five

Duration: 60–140 minutes on the computer

Materials: *Kid Pix 2* Slide Show Planning Sheet (page 123), science notes, Water Cycle Performance Assessment (page 124) optional

Procedure:

Before the Computer:

Teaching the water cycle allows for hands-on activities involving evaporation (drying paint) and condensation (ice water and steam condensation). Use hands-on experiments to introduce these concepts.

Teacher Resource for Weather/Water Experiments:

Sherwood, Williams, and Rockwell. *More Mudpies to Magnets: Science for Young Children.* Gryphon House, Inc., 1990.

• Steps of the water cycle (according to your resources; you may modify these steps)

— Heat from the sun makes the water from the land and seas evaporate. Moist air rises and cools.

— As water rises into the cold air, it condenses into tiny drops of water. When millions of drops of water join together, they form clouds.

— Clouds rise and cool further. Water droplets get bigger. When water drops become large enough and heavy enough, they fall as rain, hail, sleet, or snow.

— Water soaks into the soil and becomes ground water. Some water runs across the surface of the land and into rivers, lakes, and oceans.

— Heat from the sun makes the water from the land and seas evaporate.

(The water cycle begins again.)

Vocabulary:

evaporation—It is water turning into invisible vapor that rises up into the atmosphere.

condensation—It is water turning back into its liquid form.

precipitation—It is water that falls from the sky in the form of rain, sleet, snow, or hail.

• Your students will plan and create their own animated versions of the water cycle.

• Have your students show the water cycle with one background only the water/weather changes in each slide.

To do this, create the background. Re-create it for each planning frame. Illustrate the water's role in each frame. Be sure the narration includes a clear explanation of what is happening. Use arrows to show the direction of the water's flow.

THE WATER CYCLE *(cont.)*

On the Computer:

- Create a title slide. Save as... Water Cycle Title.

- Create your background slide. Save it as background. It is good to keep a copy of this saved in case the background is altered beyond recovery.

- Add the first step of the water cycle. Show the direction of the water's evaporation, using arrows. Clearly illustrate the path of the water. Save this slide as evaporation.

Kid Pix Stamps:

Hint: To change the direction of the arrow stamp in *Kid Pix 2*, click on the arrow stamp. Select Edit Stamp from the Goodies menu. This takes you into the Stamp Editor. Here you can change the direction of the arrows by clicking on the arrows on the right side of the dialogue box. (You can also change the color, size, and shape of the stamp here.) When you are satisfied with the changes you have made, click OK. The stamp will remain altered until you go back to the Stamp Editor and select Restore Original.

Stamp Editor:

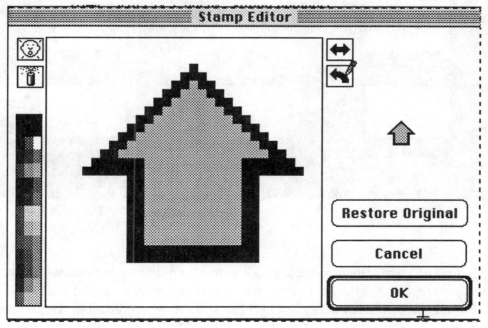

Important Note:

If your students are all saving their slide shows to the same place and they give them the same names, they will replace each other's slides (completely delete the previous slide of the same name and replace it with the new one) each time they save a slide with the same name. You cannot have two Water Cycle Title slides in the same place. It is important to create a separate folder for each student or to use disks to store slide shows, or to include initials at the end of each document name.

THE WATER CYCLE *(cont.)*

- Select Open from the File menu. Open the background slide again. Illustrate the second step of the water cycle, the moist air rising and forming clouds. Save this slide as condensation.

- Open the background slide again. Show the water returning to the land in the form of precipitation (rain), snow, sleet, or hail. Save this slide as precipitation.

- As you open the background slide this time, show how the water seeps into the ground and runs off into rivers, lakes, and oceans. Save this slide as ground water.

- Put the slides into a slide show. To show the perpetual continuation of the cycle, when you play it, select Play Looped from the Goodies menu or press the play looped button at the bottom of the screen.

Play Looped

Options:

You can put all of your student slide shows together to play as one giant water cycle to show how the water cycle repeats itself. To do this, create a folder on your hard drive called "Class Water Cycle." Put all student slides in here. Open the slide show application. Begin putting the slides in the program in order. It does not matter if all of one student's slides are together, as long as the steps of the water cycle are shown. Continue putting slides into the slide show until all slides have been used. Play this as one big slide show.

Note: If you wish to do this, your students must name their slides differently (e.g., putting their initials at the end of each slide.) Otherwise, each time you add a new group of slides, they will replace the old ones with the same names.

THE WATER CYCLE *(cont.)*

KID PIX SLIDE SHOW PLANNING SHEET

Title Slide

Buttons/Links: _____

Notes (Text/Sounds/Animations): _____

Slide 1

Buttons/Links: _____

Notes (Text/Sounds/Animations): _____

Slide 2

Buttons/Links: _____

Notes (Text/Sounds/Animations): _____

Slide 3

Buttons/Links: _____

Notes (Text/Sounds/Animations): _____

Slide 4

Buttons/Links: _____

Notes (Text/Sounds/Animations): _____

Slide 5

Buttons/Links: _____

Notes (Text/Sounds/Animations): _____

THE WATER CYCLE *(cont.)*

THE WATER CYCLE PERFORMANCE ASSESSMENT

Student Name: _____

The water cycle slide show contains a **title slide.**

Not Yet   Almost There   I Did It!   Above and Beyond

The water cycle slide show clearly shows **evaporation.**

Not Yet   Almost There   I Did It!   Above and Beyond

Condensation is clearly demonstrated in the water cycle slide show.

Not Yet   Almost There   I Did It!   Above and Beyond

The **precipitation** step is explained in the water cycle slide show.

Not Yet   Almost There   I Did It!   Above and Beyond

The water cycle slide show tells about **ground water and runoff water.**

Not Yet   Almost There   I Did It!   Above and Beyond

The student used **creativity and detail** in the slide show.

Not Yet   Almost There   I Did It!   Above and Beyond

Notes: _____

I really liked _____

I recommend _____

GRAPH THE GROWTH

Help your students make professional looking line graphs to enhance their hands-on science experiments.

Grade Level: three to five

Duration: 30–45 minutes on the computer

Materials: bean seeds, soil, containers, science journal or notes, Science Experiment Form (page 127), Plant Growth Observation Chart (page 128), *ClarisWorks* or another integrated software package

Procedure:

Before the Computer:

- As your students learn what plants need to survive, involve them in a hands-on experiment to see how denying a plant what it needs to sustain life will have serious effects.

- Have your students fill out their science experiment form to plan their group's experiments.

- Each student or group of students has two plants. One plant is the control plant that will be given food, water, sunlight, fertilizer, etc. This plant should show a normal plant's growth pattern. The second plant will either be denied something it needs to live or given too much of it (too much water, too much fertilizer, a heat lamp 24 hours a day). Allow your students to decide what variable they will change and how.

- Have your students take notes on their plant activity, using the Plant Growth Observation Chart.

- At the end of the observation period, have your students use *ClarisWorks* to make a line graph of their results.

On the Computer:

Have your students take their Plant Growth Observation Charts to the computer. There they can use the information in their charts to set up spreadsheets in *ClarisWorks*.

Instructions:

— Double click on *ClarisWorks*.

— Select a spreadsheet document and click OK.

— In cell A1, type the title of your graph.

Options:

- Use the same strategies to graph any information gathered by your student scientists.

- Use the above lesson plan to graph your students favorite type of music or how they spend their days.

	A	B	C	D	E	F	G
1	Plant Growth Comparison	Control Plant	Plant with No Sun				
2	Day 1	0	1				
3	Day 3	1	1				
4	Day 5	2	2				
5	Day 8	4	3				
6	Day 10	5	3				
7	Day 12	6	3				
8	Day 15	8	3				
9	Day 17	10	3				
10	Day 19	10	2				
11	Day 22	12	2				
12	Day 24	13	2				
13	Day 26	14	2				

Plant Growth Comparison

▨ Control Plant
■ Plant with No Sun

GRAPH THE GROWTH *(cont.)*

— Beginning in cell A2, type in the days that the you observed your plant.

— Column B will be your control plant. Type in the height of the plant at each day you observed it. Do not enter anything except the numbers (cm, inches, etc.). Entering other information will affect your graph.

— Column C will be your variable plant. Type in the height of the plant at each day you observed it. Do not enter anything except the numbers (cm, inches, etc.). Entering other information will affect your graph.

— Drag your cursor across your information to select (highlight) it.

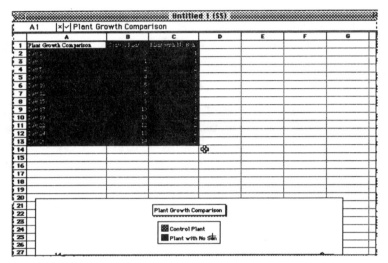

— Select Make Chart from the Options: menu.

— Select the type of chart you wish to make, in this case, a line graph.

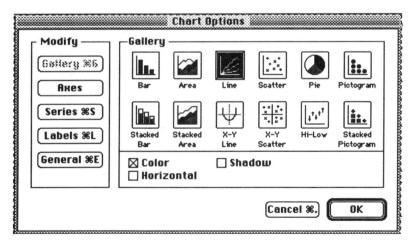

— Go to Axes to name your X and Y axis.

— Edit your title with Labels.

— If you wish to change your symbols or symbol colors, go to Series.

— Use your graphics tools to change the colors of your graph.

— Change the position and appearance of your legend in Labels.

GRAPH THE GROWTH *(cont.)*

SCIENCE EXPERIMENT FORM

Science Project Title: _____

Question: What do we want to find out?

_____

_____

Hypothesis: What do we think we will find out?

_____

_____

_____

Materials:

_____

_____

_____

_____

Procedure: How will we find out? List step-by-step instructions.

    1. _____

    2. _____

    3. _____

    4. _____

    5. _____

Results: What actually happened?

_____

_____

_____

Conclusion: What did we learn?

_____

_____

_____

_____

GRAPH THE GROWTH *(cont.)*

PLANT GROWTH OBSERVATION CHART

As you observe the growth patterns of your plants, record the information here.

Date	Day#	Control Plant	Experimental Plant	Notes

INVENTORS AND INVENTIONS

Incredible inventions have changed the way we live, from electricity to the telephone. Help your students learn about the people who made it happen with this *HyperStudio* project.

Grade Level: four to five

Duration: 60–190 minutes on the computer

Materials: research, Inventor Research Sheet (page 131), *HyperStudio* Planning Sheet (page 132), *HyperStudio* software, Inventors and Inventions Performance Assessment (page 133)

Procedure:

Before the Computer:

- As you study significant inventions, allow each student to choose one inventor to highlight.

- As part of a mini-research project, each student will find background information about the inventor, along with taking a close look at the invention itself.

- Have your students use the Inventor Research Sheet to help them organize their notes. The *HyperStudio* Stack Planning Sheet will also help your students plan in advance before working on the computer.

On the Computer:

Title Card Categories:

Inventor Name

- — Biographical information (early life, education, career, family)
- — Invention (diagram of invention, animation if desired)
- — Significance

Hint: If this is your class' first *HyperStudio* project, you could set up the shell of the stack your students are going to create. To do this, you must create the title card, put the buttons in place, and create the cards (blank) that they need to be linked to. You can even create the text fields for your students. Save it as Inventor/Invention Stack.

- If you use computer disks, just load a copy onto each student's disk.

- If you are all operating off of one classroom computer, save the first stack as "Inventor/Invention Stack." Then, Save As...Inventor/Invention 1, Save As...Inventor/Invention 2, and so on. Continue to do this until you have a stack for each student. Assign them a number. They will work on the coordinating stack.

- Now all students must do is enter the information and decorate.

Options:

- Create one inventor/inventions title card with all possible inventors (all student projects) listed as buttons and link all stacks together. Now you have an interactive inventor encyclopedia for future use.

- If you do not have *HyperStudio* or a similar program, this also makes a great *Kid Pix 2* Slide Show. Just make a slide or two for each category.

- This is a great springboard into your students' own inventions. Extend the unit by having your students create their inventions—something that they could use in everyday life. They can create *HyperStudio* stacks about themselves.

INVENTORS AND INVENTIONS (cont.)

INVENTORS

Nicolas Appert	Willis Carrier	Laurens Hammond
Edwin Armstrong	Edmund Cartwright	Joseph Marie Jacquard
John Logie Baird	Samuel Colt	Charles Franklin Kettering
Alexander Graham Bell	Gottlieb Daimler	Samuel B. Morse
Vincent Bendix	John Frederic Daniell	Alfred Nobel
Karl Benz	Melville Dewey	Isaac M. Singer
Emile Berliner	John Ericsson	Elmer Ambrose Sperry
James Bogardus	Benjamin Franklin	Joseph Wilson Swann
Louis Braille	William Friese-Greene	James Watt
Joseph Bramah	Robert Fulton	George Westinghouse
John Moses Browning	Dennis Gabor	Robert Whitehead
William S. Burroughs	Peter Carl Goldmark	Eli Whitney
David Bushnell	Charles Goodyear	Sir Frank Whittle
W. H. Carothers	Elisha Gray	

INVENTORS AND INVENTIONS *(cont.)*

Name: _____   Date: _____

Due Date: _____

INVENTOR RESEARCH SHEET

_____
(inventor)

Biographical information (early life, education, family, career) _____

_____

_____

_____

_____

_____

Invention

Diagram

```
┌─────────────────────────────────────────────────┐
│                                                 │
│                                                 │
│                                                 │
│                                                 │
│                                                 │
│                                                 │
│                                                 │
│                                                 │
│                                                 │
└─────────────────────────────────────────────────┘
```

Description _____

_____

_____

_____

Significance

_____

_____

_____

_____

_____

INVENTORS AND INVENTIONS *(cont.)*

HYPERSTUDIO PLANNING SHEET

Title Card

Buttons/Links: _____

Notes (Text/Sounds/Animations): _____
_____
_____

Card 1

Buttons/Links: _____

Notes (Text/Sounds/Animations): _____
_____
_____

Card 2

Buttons/Links: _____

Notes (Text/Sounds/Animations): _____
_____
_____

Card 3

Buttons/Links: _____

Notes (Text/Sounds/Animations): _____
_____
_____

Card 4

Buttons/Links: _____

Notes (Text/Sounds/Animations): _____
_____
_____

Card 5

Buttons/Links: _____

Notes (Text/Sounds/Animations): _____
_____
_____

INVENTORS AND INVENTIONS *(cont.)*

Student Name: _____

INVENTORS AND INVENTIONS PERFORMANCE ASSESSMENT

The inventor stack was **well planned and well organized.**

Not Yet   Almost There   I Did It!   Above and Beyond

The inventor project contains information about the inventor's life.

Not Yet   Almost There   I Did It!   Above and Beyond

The **invention** was detailed, with a diagram and description.

Not Yet   Almost There   I Did It!   Above and Beyond

The **significance** of the inventor and his invention was clearly explained.

Not Yet   Almost There   I Did It!   Above and Beyond

The student used **creativity and detail** in the project.

Not Yet   Almost There   I Did It!   Above and Beyond

I really liked _____

_____

_____

I recommend _____

_____

_____

BODY SYSTEMS

Your students will create an interactive diagram of the body systems.

Grade Level: four to five

Duration: 60–180 minutes on the computer (depending on how specific it is)

Materials: Body Systems Organizer (page 135), *HyperStudio* Planning Sheet (page 136), research CD-ROMs (e.g., A.D.A.M, The Family Doctor, etc.)

Procedure:

Before the Computer:

As your students begin their study of the body systems, introduce this project. Introducing it at the beginning can improve motivation for the unit. It will be a way for them to organize their notes and all that they learn into a multimedia presentation.

On the Computer:

- Have your students create *HyperStudio* stacks from their notes.

    Title Card: The Body Systems

    Circulatory

    Nervous

    Digestive

    Muscular

    Skeletal

    Respiratory

    Reproductive (optional)

- Each body system card should include the parts of that body system and its purpose.

- As your students learn the parts and the purpose of each system, they increase the available information in their *HyperStudio* stacks.

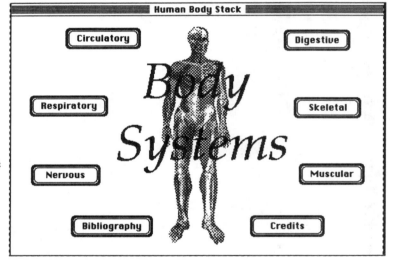

Options:

If this project is too large for your students, break it down. Allow each student to create a project about a single body system or even a single organ. It will make the project more manageable while allowing your students to specialize on the body system that most interests them.

BODY SYSTEMS *(cont.)*

THE BODY SYSTEMS ORGANIZER

Use this sheet to organize your notes about the body's systems.

Circulatory System

Parts:

_____

Function:

_____

Nervous System

Parts:

_____

Function:

_____

Digestive System

Parts:

_____

Function:

_____

Muscular System

Parts:

_____

Function:

_____

Skeletal System

Parts:

_____

Function:

_____

Respiratory System

Parts:

_____

Function:

_____

BODY SYSTEMS *(cont.)*

HYPERSTUDIO PLANNING SHEET

Title Card

Buttons/Links: _____

Notes (Text/Sounds/Animations): _____

Card 1

Buttons/Links: _____

Notes (Text/Sounds/Animations): _____

Card 2

Buttons/Links: _____

Notes (Text/Sounds/Animations): _____

Card 3

Buttons/Links: _____

Notes (Text/Sounds/Animations): _____

Card 4

Buttons/Links: _____

Notes (Text/Sounds/Animations): _____

Card 5

Buttons/Links: _____

Notes (Text/Sounds/Animations): _____

MY SCIENCE PROJECT

Present science projects in a new way—on the computer. Use *HyperStudio* to create an impressive lab report.

Grade Level: four to five

Duration: 120–240 minutes on the computer

Materials: planned science project, Science Project Summary Sheet (page 138), *HyperStudio* Planning Sheet (page 139)

Procedure:

Before the Computer:

As part of a science unit, your students will plan and perform their own science experiments. The experiments will be presented on a *HyperStudio* Stack.

On the Computer:

- Your students can begin their *HyperStudio* stacks even before their science projects are complete. Once your students have chosen topics, they can set up the organization of their stacks, including the title pages and the cards that will support their experiments. Set the expectations about what must be included. It will be helpful to use the planning form provided, but some students may not be ready for a complete science project.

- Those who do research or have extensive graphs or supporting information may want to include an additional category called "Supporting Data." As they complete each portion, they can add the information on the cards.

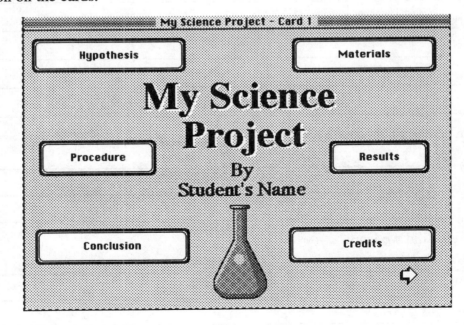

Options:

For beginners or younger students, use *Kid Pix 2* Slide Show to present their science projects. Use one slide for each portion of the project (a hypothesis slide, a materials slide, etc.).

MY SCIENCE PROJECT *(cont.)*

SCIENCE PROJECT SUMMARY SHEET

Science Project Title: _____

Question: What do we want to find out?

_____

_____

Hypothesis: What do we think we will find out?

_____

_____

_____

Materials:

_____

_____

_____

_____

Procedure: How will we find out? List step-by-step instructions.

  1. _____

  2. _____

  3. _____

  4. _____

  5. _____

Results: What actually happened?

_____

_____

_____

Conclusion: What did we learn?

_____

_____

_____

_____

MY SCIENCE PROJECT *(cont.)*

HYPERSTUDIO PLANNING SHEET

Title Card

Buttons/Links: _____

Notes (Text/Sounds/Animations): _____

Card 1

Buttons/Links: _____

Notes (Text/Sounds/Animations): _____

Card 2

Buttons/Links: _____

Notes (Text/Sounds/Animations): _____

Card 3

Buttons/Links: _____

Notes (Text/Sounds/Animations): _____

Card 4

Buttons/Links: _____

Notes (Text/Sounds/Animations): _____

Card 5

Buttons/Links: _____

Notes (Text/Sounds/Animations): _____

¡HOLA!

Help your students learn foreign vocabulary by making a living dictionary of their new words.

Grade Level: three to five

Duration: 30–60 minutes on the computer

Materials: vocabulary words, Vocabulary Word Slide Show Planning Sheet (page 142), *Kid Pix 2*

Before the Computer:

- As your students learn new vocabulary in a foreign language, you can create fantastic slide shows that act as reinforcements and even tutors for your class.

- Each student will be responsible for at least one word, which will require two slides. The slide show will be created in a "quiz" fashion so your students can test their own vocabulary knowledge. Each vocabulary word will have a slide with the word in English and a coordinating illustration. There will be a second slide that gives the Spanish translation and the correct pronunciation. (Your students may need help remembering this.)

Example:

> Slide 3
>
> "What is the number one in Spanish?"
>
> Slide 4
>
> "uno"
>
> Slide 5
>
> "What is the color blue in Spanish?"
>
> Slide 6
>
> "azul"

- Use the optional planning sheet to prepare students ahead of time. You can even help them with the pronunciation by giving them the phonetic spellings of their words.

File Edit Goodies

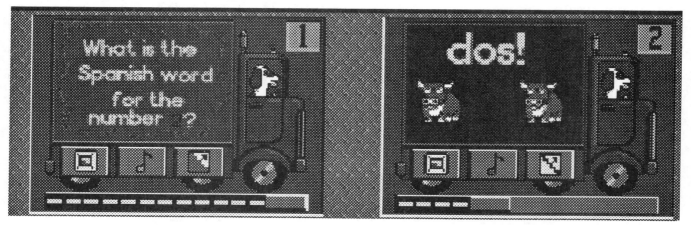

¡HOLA! *(cont.)*

On the Computer:

- Your students can use the slide show portion of *Kid Pix 2* to create their two (or more) slides.

- In a lab setting:
  - Each student saves his/her slides to a disk. All slides are compiled onto the hard drive of the classroom computer where one slide show is created from all students' slides.
  - The completed slide show can then be loaded onto each student's individual disk.

- On a single classroom computer:
  - All slides are saved onto the hard drive where one slide show is created from all students' slides.
  - Have a student put the final slide show together.

Hint:

To make the "quiz" portion work even better, lengthen the question slide to the maximum number of seconds. During the slide show, advance to the next slide after thinking of the word, the student needs only to click the mouse. Therefore, if a student knows the word, he/she can bypass the remaining seconds and get to the next slide.

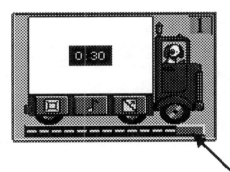

Lengthen slide pause time by dragging this tool to its maximum "highway length."

Options:

- There are many ways to organize this activity. It can be an individual activity; students can create their own slide shows by making multiple slides and putting them together.

- Create a new slide show (or just add more to the old ones) for each unit.

- Do not limit your vocabulary slide shows to foreign language. You can use spelling words, social studies words, science words, or anything you can think of.

Early Finishers

Have those early finishers in your class create the following additional slides:

- title slide
- introduction slide (explaining the purpose of the slide show and how it works)
- ending slide

¡HOLA! *(cont.)*

Student Name: _____

Teacher: _____

VOCABULARY WORD SLIDE SHOW PLANNING SHEET

Word: _____

Meaning _____

Slide #1

Slide #2

FAMOUS ARTISTS

Research the masters and increase your students' awareness of art history.

Grade Level: four to five

Duration: 70–130 minutes on the computer

Materials: research CD-ROMs (e.g., *Grolier's Encyclopedia, Encarta, Art Gallery*), other reference materials, research notes, *HyperStudio* Planning Sheet (page 145)

Procedure:

Before the Computer:

- As part of an art class or art appreciation unit, take a look at artists who have influenced our lives.

- Information to be included in the stack:
    - artist's name
    - birth/death
    - biographical information
    - great works

- Link all of these together into one fantastic art appreciation resource for your classroom.

On the Computer:

Have your students use their notes and their *HyperStudio* Planning Sheet to create multimedia presentations about the artists they chose.

Options:

- Do a similar project about famous musicians.

- Have a fine arts night to show parents the importance of the program at your school.

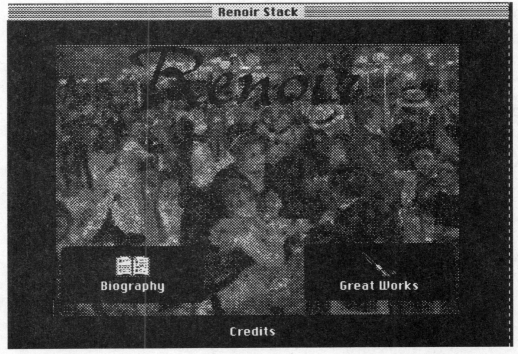

FAMOUS ARTISTS *(cont.)*

POSSIBLE ARTISTS TO CHOOSE FROM

Giovanni Bellini	Donatello	Pierre Auguste Renoir
Sandro Botticelli	Jan van Eyck	Raphael (Raffaello Sanzio)
Brunelleschi (Filippo)	Lorenzo Ghiberti	Hugo van der Goes
Mary Cassatt	Paul Gauguin	Vincent Van Gogh
Paul Cezanne	Frans Hals	Rembrandt van Rijn
Christo	Edouard Manet	Diego Velazaquez
Leonardo da Vinci	Michelangelo	Jan Vermeer
Salvador Dali	Claude Monet	Andy Warhol
Edgar Degas	Pablo Picasso	Andrew Wyeth

FAMOUS ARTISTS *(cont.)*

HYPERSTUDIO PLANNING SHEET

Card 2

Buttons/Links: _____

Notes (Text/Sounds/Animations): _____

Card 5

Buttons/Links: _____

Notes (Text/Sounds/Animations): _____

Card 1

Buttons/Links: _____

Notes (Text/Sounds/Animations): _____

Card 4

Buttons/Links: _____

Notes (Text/Sounds/Animations): _____

Title Card

Buttons/Links: _____

Notes (Text/Sounds/Animations): _____

Card 3

Buttons/Links: _____

Notes (Text/Sounds/Animations): _____

SPORTS

Extend your students' physical education by taking a closer look at their favorite sports.

Grade Level: three to five

Duration: 70–120 minutes on the computer

Materials: reference materials, Sports Research Sheet (page 147), *HyperStudio* Planning Sheet (page 148)

Procedure:

Before the Computer:

- Have your students choose sports to research. This can be a sport they are currently playing in P.E. or just a sport that interests them.

- Using the Sports Research Sheet provided, guide your students toward finding plenty of information about their sports. If you are involved in a study about a particular country or area of the world, encourage some of your students to take a look at their national sports.

Examples of national sports: baseball, basketball, aerial sports, tennis, field and ice hockey, football, bullfighting, archery, gymnastics, golf, automobile racing, ice skating, boxing, soccer, rugby, cricket, martial arts, diving, horse racing, skiing, track and field, weight lifting, and wrestling

Examples of Olympic Sports

Winter:

Alpine and Nordic skiing, biathlon, ice hockey, figure skating, speed skating, bobsledding, and luge

Summer:

archery, basketball, boxing, canoeing and kayaking, cycling, equestrian arts, fencing, field hockey, gymnastics, handball, judo, modern pentathlon, rowing, shooting, soccer, swimming, diving, synchronized swimming, track and field, volleyball, water polo, weight lifting, wrestling, and yachting

Have your students use a *HyperStudio* Planning Sheet to organize their research.

On the Computer:

Have your students use their notes and their *HyperStudio* Planning Sheet to create multimedia presentations about the sports they chose.

Options:

Link all of these *HyperStudio* stacks together to create a wonderful classroom resource—a multimedia stack about all kinds of sports.

SPORTS *(cont.)*

SPORTS RESEARCH SHEET

Sport: _____

History of the Sport (how and where it started):

_____

_____

_____

_____

Necessary Equipment (include the clothing and field/court):

_____

_____

_____

Rules and Regulations:

_____

_____

_____

_____

Famous Contests of this Sport:

_____

_____

_____

Famous Players:

_____

_____

_____

SPORTS *(cont.)*

HYPERSTUDIO PLANNING SHEET

Title Card

Buttons/Links: _____

Notes (Text/Sounds/Animations): _____

Card 1

Buttons/Links: _____

Notes (Text/Sounds/Animations): _____

Card 2

Buttons/Links: _____

Notes (Text/Sounds/Animations): _____

Card 3

Buttons/Links: _____

Notes (Text/Sounds/Animations): _____

Card 4

Buttons/Links: _____

Notes (Text/Sounds/Animations): _____

Card 5

Buttons/Links: _____

Notes (Text/Sounds/Animations): _____

PUZZLING STUDENTS

Help your students get to know each other at the beginning of the year by having them create puzzles about themselves and their interests.

Grade Level: two to five

Duration: 20–45 minutes on the computer

Materials: an envelope for each student, construction paper, *Kid Pix 2*

Procedure:

Before the Computer:

- Have your students create puzzles that introduce themselves and their hobbies to their new classmates.

- Encourage your students to be creative and use lots of colors and pictures.

On the Computer:

- Have your students create pictures about themselves, showing some of the activities they enjoy doing. Make sure they put their names on the pictures. Each picture will be printed out.

- Using the wacky pencil, puzzle piece lines are drawn onto the pictures. Each picture is printed a second time.

After the Computer

- Each student mounts both of his/her pictures onto colored construction paper for support. (You may want to laminate these.)

- Each student then cuts the picture with drawn puzzle pieces into actual pieces and puts the pieces into an envelope. The other picture, still intact, is given back to you. These pictures are put into a folder to use as answer keys to the puzzles.

- Place all of the envelopes into a shoe box. The puzzles can be reconstructed as a structured activity or used as an independent activity in a reading corner or center.

Options:

This would make a neat bulletin board . . . "Mrs. Carter's Puzzling Students."

WELCOME TO OUR SCHOOL

Help your students learn about the faculty, staff, and facility at your school site while creating a wonderful resource for school visitors.

Grade Level: three to five

Duration: 120+ minutes on the computer

Materials: *HyperStudio,* Special People in Our School (page 151), school map, school statistics/information, *Quick Take Camera* (optional) or scanner

Procedure:

Before the Computer:

- To complete this project properly, lots of research will be needed, and it must all be done as accurately as possible. You may want to scale down or even increase the size of this project, based on how you wish to use it in your school. The hardest part of this project will be assigning the different responsibilities.

- Make a list of everything you wish to include. Have your students help with this task. They will have lots of ideas you might have missed.

- List all school personnel to be included. Make sure you write down the different areas to do special reports on, as well, such as the playground, gym, cafeteria, media center, etc.

  Suggested Topics:
  - principal, assistant principal, etc.
  - teachers
  - paraprofessionals
  - other special people
  - nurse, office staff, cafeteria people, janitorial staff, etc.

- Give your students guidelines as they gather their information.

- Use the interview form provided (or one similar) to make sure that all students acquire the same information.

- Come up with questions that interest your students for the optional questions. They may want to know about pets or what that person wanted to be when they were young, etc.

- Use your digital camera (e.g., *Quick Take Camera* by Apple) or scan in pictures so that anyone can recognize the special people and places in your school.

On the Computer:

- There are several ways to organize this project. If you are attempting to do it on one computer in your classroom, you can create one stack and have your students work at the computer to add their particular cards. If you are doing it in a lab or mini-lab situation, your students may have to create their own stacks and when finished put them all on one disk and have someone link them appropriately. You may want to elect one person who understands *HyperStudio* and is organized to be in charge of creating the backbone and introductions of the project.

Options:

- Have your students create a *Kid Pix 2* slide show about their school and its facility.

- Let your students publish a book, using a program such as *EasyBook,* about your school.

WELCOME TO OUR SCHOOL *(cont.)*

SPECIAL PEOPLE IN OUR SCHOOL

Name: _____

Job at Our School: _____

Educational Background: _____

Interests/Hobbies: _____

_____

Special Interest Questions (e.g., best part of your job, biggest challenge, etc.)

1. How did you get involved in education?

_____

_____

_____

2. _____

_____

_____

3. _____

_____

_____

4. _____

_____

_____

SOFTWARE SHORTCUTS

The next several pages contain software hints to help you use the recommended software in this book. The tips that are given are quite often taken from a manual or previous teacher and student experiences.

Hints for Using Software Shortcuts:

- Copy the software shortcuts and put them in a binder near your computer.

- Make copies of the software shortcuts for your Software Hints/Staff Development Binder. Make these available to teachers as alternatives to a manual.

- Copy these pages on colored paper. Laminate them and keep them next to your classroom computer for easy access for teachers and students.

- Make these sheets available to your students when they are working on technology projects.

TEACHER HINTS FOR USING KID PIX 2

- Do not feel like you need to spend a great deal of time teaching your students about all of the tools. Instead, show them a few of the basics (changing colors, using different tool options) and then let them explore on their own.

- There are many hidden tricks and effects in *Kid Pix 2* that you can find by using the option or shift key. Encourage your students to try to find them and share them with others.

- Post a large piece of chart paper next to the computer. Each time a student finds a helpful hint, have him add it to the chart (which is visible from the computer[s]) so that each time a student goes to the computer, he can see the latest discoveries.

- If your computer time is limited, use planning sheets (or student notes) to plan ahead for *Kid Pix 2* projects. It really improves time spent on the task at a computer.

- Sound takes up a lot of memory. If you do not have a lot of memory (on a disk or your hard drive), have your students use sound only when necessary.

- When printing, have your students avoid solid color backgrounds. Although they add to a picture, they can really use up a color printer ribbon. It also takes much longer to print. Use color backgrounds in slide shows, not in pictures you are going to print.

- Let your students teach each other. Have a technology share time (maybe five minutes) each day where a student can share a great project or a neat *Kid Pix 2* trick.

KID PIX 2 SHORTCUTS

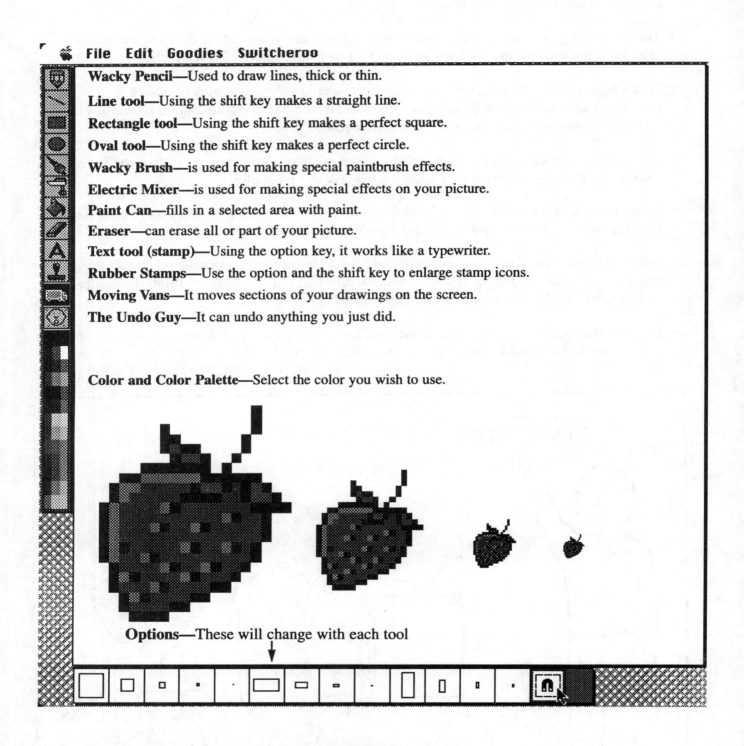

File   Edit   Goodies   Switcheroo

Wacky Pencil—Used to draw lines, thick or thin.

Line tool—Using the shift key makes a straight line.

Rectangle tool—Using the shift key makes a perfect square.

Oval tool—Using the shift key makes a perfect circle.

Wacky Brush—is used for making special paintbrush effects.

Electric Mixer—is used for making special effects on your picture.

Paint Can—fills in a selected area with paint.

Eraser—can erase all or part of your picture.

Text tool (stamp)—Using the option key, it works like a typewriter.

Rubber Stamps—Use the option and the shift key to enlarge stamp icons.

Moving Vans—It moves sections of your drawings on the screen.

The Undo Guy—It can undo anything you just did.

Color and Color Palette—Select the color you wish to use.

Options—These will change with each tool

KID PIX 2 SLIDE SHOW

Creating Your Slides:

Begin in *Kid Pix*. Select the program icon (double click if you are at the Finder). Draw the title slide or the first slide in your slide show. Add color and sound. Use the Tips for Creating a Good Slide Show (page 157).

Save As... Slide 1

Go to File...New (, -N)

Draw the next slide. Record the sound. Save As... Slide 2.

(When animating, Save As... Slide 1. Then make the changes—skip the file new step. Then Save As... Slide 2.)

Hint: When saving more than one slide show to a disk, give the file name another modifier, such as Egypt Slide 1, etc.

Hint: Sound and detail take up lots of room on a disk. Plan to put only one or two small slide shows on each disk.

When all slides are completed, go to Switcheroo menu and select Switch to Slide Show.

KID PIX 2 SLIDE SHOW *(cont.)*

You will see rows of three trucks with icons at the bottom. Each truck has three symbols on it: (1) Pick a Slide (it looks like a picture frame), (2) Pick a Sound (music note), and (3) the transition button.

- Click on the Pick a Slide (the first) icon. It should open your disk or folder and show you the contents of that disk or folder (all of your slides).

- Click on the slide you want and then select it. It will show a miniature version of your slide in the truck.

- Select the slides for each consecutive "truck" until all slides are in place. To quickly check the order of the slides, press the Play (like on a tape recorder) button at the bottom of the screen.

- Next click on the Pick a Sound button. Choose the sound you want and click Select. If you recorded in *Kid Pix*, that recording will automatically be chosen unless you tell it otherwise. If you want to record in slide show, click on the music note and then click the microphone. Record as you would in *Kid Pix*. Click on Save and then Select. You cannot have more than one sound on a slide unless you put the slide in more than one truck.

- Now choose your transition. Click on the transition button. Choose the one you want and then click Select. (The dissolve and the cut transitions are best when creating animation.)

- When you are finished, go to the File menu and select Save As. Name your slide show and click Save. (You can also save your slide show as a "StandAlone" slide show. This makes it possible to play the slide show without the *Kid Pix* application. Also, if you save it as a Quick Time movie, you can transport it into *ClarisWorks* or another application. Save it as a normal Slide Show first so that you can make changes later.)

- You can choose a background color for your slide show by going into the Goodies menu and selecting Background Color.

- To play your slide show, go to the Goodies menu and select Play Once or click the play button at the bottom of the screen. To play the slide show over and over, go to the Goodies menu and select Play Looped. This will play your slide show until the mouse is double clicked.

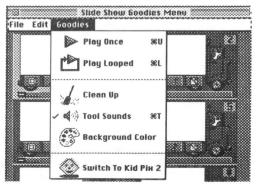

KID PIX 2 SLIDE SHOW *(cont.)*

TIPS FOR CREATING A SLIDE SHOW

Students need guidance to create good graphic presentations. This guide was created using recommendations from art and computer specialists. Share these tips with your students at the beginning of each slide show. You will be amazed at the results.

1. COLOR, COLOR, COLOR

Use colorful backgrounds. Instead of using a plain white background behind a landscape or setting, try a solid color (blue for sky, yellow for bright sun, or orange at sunset). Inside a room, use a pattern for wallpaper. Add interest but do not take away from the focus of your picture.

Use contrasting colors. Students sometimes favor similar colors and put light pink letters on a lavender background, which makes them difficult to read. Put a bright yellow on a deep red and notice the effect.

2. LARGER THAN LIFE

Draw pictures that take up the entire screen or even go off the screen. Make the most important part of your slide clear at first glance.

Example:

3. CLEAR AND EASY TO READ

Make the text part of the slide show big and bold. Use a text style that is easy to read (not too fancy).

4. LET'S HEAR IT FOR SOUND

When recording, do not accept poor quality. If you make a mistake during the recording, start over. Try to eliminate as much background noise as possible.

5. PERSONALIZE IT

Use your own artwork. Include clip art and stamps where they are needed but take ownership of your slide show by creating artwork that only you can produce.

HYPERSTUDIO

Tools:

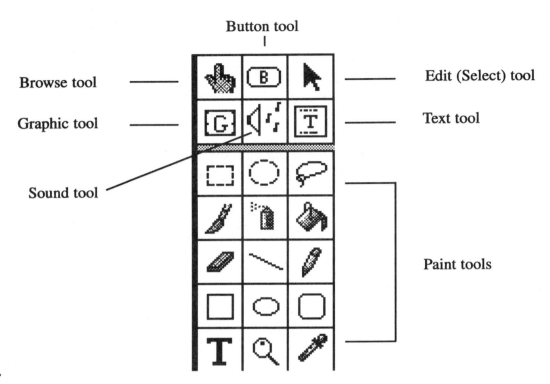

Button tool

Browse tool ——— Edit (Select) tool

Graphic tool ——— Text tool

Sound tool

Paint tools

Menu Bar

All of these pulldown menus help you navigate and create in your stack.

 File Edit Move Tools Objects Colors Options Extras

Quick Tips:

       Command-S—Saves your stack (File Menu)

       Command-B—Adds a button (Objects Menu)

       Command-G—Adds a graphic item (Objects Menu)

       Command-T—Adds a text box (Objects Menu)

       Command-L—Adds a movie or video (Objects Menu)

       Command-N—Creates a new card (Edit Menu)

"Painting Your Card"

- Choose a background color for your card/stack. You do not have to have one, but it adds interest.

- Add Clip Art from the File menu; it allows you to add graphics from a disk onto your card.

- New Card (Command-N) in the Edit menu creates a new, blank card following the current one. You can use Ready Made cards that have neat backgrounds that are already in the Edit menu.

HYPERSTUDIO *(cont.)*

The Move menu helps you navigate around your stack before you have created all of your buttons.

```
Move  Tools   Objects
   Back              ⌘~
   Home              ⌘H
   First Card        ⌘1
   Previous Card     ⌘<
   Next Card         ⌘>
   Last Card         ⌘9
   Jump To Card...   ⌘J
   Find Text...      ⌘F
```

Adding Objects to Your Card:

The Object menu helps you add text, buttons, movies, etc., to your stack. For example, just go to Add a Button in the Object menu to add a navigational or effect button. The program will then lead you through the steps to make your button work. The same goes for text, graphic items, movies, and sounds.

```
Objects  Colors   Options   Ex
   Item Info...            ⌘I
   Card Info...
   Background Info...
   Stack Info...

   Bring Closer           ⌘+
   Send Farther           ⌘~

   Add a Button...        ⌘B
   Add a Graphic Item...  ⌘G
   Add a Text Item...     ⌘T
   Add a Movie or Video...⌘L
```

Each time you add a new object to your card, *HyperStudio* will lead you through the necessary steps (selecting style, placement, actions, etc.) to make your object work.

Check Out Your Stack

Extras—Storyboard is a great way to get an overview of your stack. Using this option you can look at all cards in your stack, rearrange them, and delete them if necessary.

THE WRITING CENTER

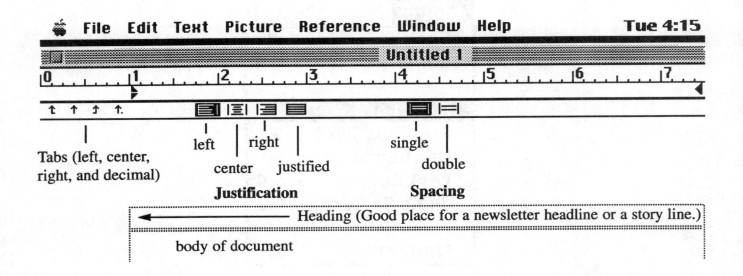

File

This allows you to do major functions that affect your whole document, such as save, print, create a new document, change your margins, quit, etc.

Edit

You can copy and paste, change your preferences, change spacing, etc.

Text

Here is where you change the way your letters look.

Picture

This menu lets you select pictures, change their sizes, crop them, rotate and flip pictures, and even give them borders.

Reference

This checks spelling and gives you access to the thesaurus.

Window

It shows you what is on your clipboard and allows you to move between open documents.

Help

This gives you additional information about the menu bar function you are using.

THE WRITING CENTER *(cont.)*

Creating Documents

When you double click on the program, you will get a dialogue box that looks like this.

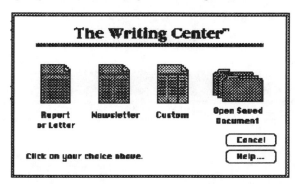

Report or Letter: Create a normal document with a body; you choose if you want a heading.

Newsletter: Creates a document with two columns and a heading.

Custom: Helps you set up a document by orientation (page setup), number of columns, and choice of heading.

Select the type of document you wish to create. If you are opening something you have already created and saved, click on Open Saved Document.

When you go to New in the File menu while working in *The Writing Center,* you will get the same dialogue box.

Setting Margins

The Writing Center automatically sets 1" (2.5 cm) margins all the way around your document. If you wish to change these margins, go to Page Setup in the File menu. Use the tab key to take you to Margin Settings. Press delete to delete 1" (2.5 cm). Type in the margins you need (e.g., ½" (1.25 cm) would be .5. Press OK.

Changing the Text Style

To change the way your letters look, go to Font in the Text menu. Here you can set the font, text style, and point size. You may set the text style for the entire document before you begin typing or change it in parts as you go by selecting the text you want to change.

Important Note: When you are working with a heading, that text is separate, so you must change it separately. What you select in the body of your document will not affect your heading and vice versa.

Adding a Picture

Go to Picture—Choose a Picture. There is a folder in *The Writing Center* Folder called Pictures. It has pictures for you to choose from in many categories. Select the category you need (Animals, Nature/Science, School, etc.), and click Open Folder. Find the picture you need and select Place in Document. Use the Picture pulldown menu to make any necessary changes to your picture. (You can also bring in your own pictures with Choose a Picture.)

CLARISWORKS 4.0

Creating a *ClarisWorks* Word Processing Document

Double click on *ClarisWorks.* If the application is open, go to New in the File menu.

Select the type of document you want to produce—Word Processing.

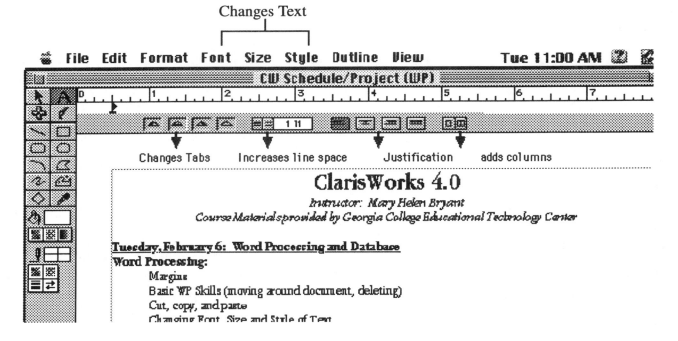

To change margins select Format from the Document menu.

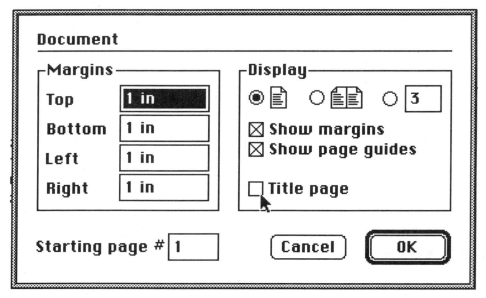

The default margins are set at 1" (2.5 cm). In order to change them, select Document from the Format menu. When the document dialog box appears, you can type in the measurements you need, (e.g., half-inch margins are set at .5). Use the tab to move from top to bottom and right to left.

CLARISWORKS 4.0 *(cont.)*

Moving Around Your Document

There are two ways in which you can move around within your word processing document.

— You can use the mouse to move around within your word processing document.
— You can use the arrow keys to move around within your word processing document.

Changing Text Font, Size, and Style

When you want or need to change a font, point size, and/or style, you need to follow three easy steps.

1. Use the mouse to highlight the desired text you wish to change.

2. Select Font, Size, and/or Format.

    a. In the Font menu you can choose Times, Helvetica, or any number of fonts that are available.

    b. In the Size menu you can choose any number between 4 and 255.

    c. In the Style menu you can choose a variety of text styles (e.g., bold, italics, underline, plain text, etc.). You can also use keyboard shortcuts to change styles.

Cut, Copy, and Paste

When you want or need to cut, copy, and/or paste a section of text, you need to follow four easy steps.

1. Use the mouse to highlight the desired text you wish to cut or copy.

2. Select Cut or Copy from the Edit menu.

3. Move your cursor to the place where you wish to insert the cut or copied text.

4. Select Paste from the Edit menu.

Tabs

There are four different types of tabs—Left, Center, Right, and Decimal.

In order to change tabs, which are automatically set at .5" (1.25 cm) left, click on the desired tab and drag it to the desired point on the ruler.

Example:

Left Tab	Center Tab	Right Tab	Decimal Tab
Student	Teacher	Grade	Supply donation
Patrice Scott	Jones	Fourth	$1.50
Blake Atkins	Loeber	Second	$.50
Jenny Bavaro	Buffington	Fifth	$12.00

Writing Tools

• Spell Check—Select Check Document Spelling from Writing Tools, which is in the Edit menu. (The keyboard shortcut is Command =.)

• Thesaurus—Highlight the word you wish to change and then select Thesaurus from Writing Tools, which is in the Edit menu. (The keyboard shortcut is Shift Command Z.)

CLARISWORKS 4.0 *(cont.)*

CLARISWORKS SPREADSHEET

Creating a Graph

1. Double click on the *ClarisWorks* application.

2. Select Spreadsheet and then click OK.

3. On the screen you will see the rows and columns of your spreadsheet. Begin by typing your information into cell address A1. The information you type will appear in the data entry box but will not be entered into the cell address until you press the return key or enter key. If you have made a mistake in a cell you have already entered, select the cell with the error and retype it. The new version will not appear until you press return or enter.

	File	**Edit**	**Form‍at**	**Calculate**	**Options**	**Uiew**

Untitled 1 (SS)

B4	× ✓	1

	A	**B**	**C**	**D**	
1	How I Spend My Day	#of hours			
2	sleeping	8			
3	working	10			
4	cooking	1			
5	reading	0.5			
6	eating	1			
7	playing/resting	4.5			
8					
9					
10					
11					
12					

4. In column A, type what you want to measure. For example, if you were going to graph favorite foods, this column would contain the different types (e.g., pizza, tacos, hamburgers, etc.). To move from cell to cell, you can use your mouse or your arrow keys. If your entries are too large to fit into your column, place your cursor at the end of the column header cells (A, B, C, etc.). When the arrow turns into a cursor, you will be able to increase the size of your columns. You can do the same thing with row sizes.

5. In column B, type your measurements. For example, if you were graphing favorite foods, this column would contain the number of votes each food received. Only numbers should be entered into this column.

6. Click and drag your mouse across all of the information you entered until everything is highlighted.

CLARISWORKS 4.0 *(cont.)*

CLARISWORKS SPREADSHEET *(cont.)*

7. Select Make Chart from the Options menu. It will give you a general menu that looks like this:

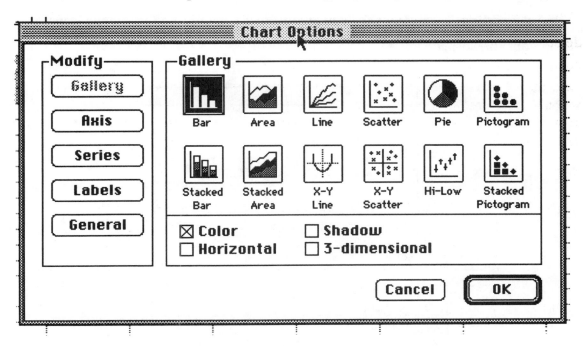

8. Select the type of graph you would like (e.g., pie, bar, etc.), and click OK.

9. To add or change a title, select Modify Chart from the Options menu and then click on labels. Axes (labels x and y axis), Series (changes appearance), Labels (adds titles, etc.), and General offers options that allow you to add or change things to your graph.

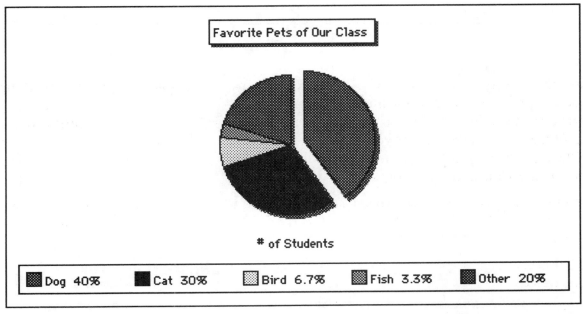

CLARISWORKS 4.0 *(cont.)*

CLARISWORKS SPREADSHEET *(cont.)*

Performing Calculations in *ClarisWorks* Spreadsheet

ClarisWorks can perform calculations for you automatically with just a few simple steps:

1. Set up your spreadsheet.

	A	B
1	Expense	Cost
2		
3	Pens	$6.50
4	Pencils	$2.20
5	Paper	$13.22
6	Diskettes	$33.25
7	Ribbons	$9.85
8		
9	Total	
10		
11	Average Expense	
12	Minimum	
13	Maximum	
14		

To set your number specifications (currency, decimals, etc.), highlight the cells you want to format and select Number from the Format menu. Click on the desired number format and then click OK.

Format Number, Date, and Time

Number
- ○ General
- ● Currency
- ○ Percent
- ○ Scientific
- ○ Fixed

- ☐ Commas
- ☐ Negatives in ()

Precision [2]

Date
- ○ 11/29/94
- ○ Nov 29, 1994
- ○ November 29, 1994
- ○ Tue, Nov 29, 1994
- ○ Tuesday, November 29, 1994

Time
- ○ 5:20 PM   ○ 17:20
- ○ 5:20:15 PM   ○ 17:20:15

[Cancel]   [OK]

CLARISWORKS 4.0 *(cont.)*

CLARISWORKS SPREADSHEET *(cont.)*

Performing Calculations in *ClarisWorks* Spreadsheet (cont.)

2. To add all of the numbers in one column, highlight where you want the total to appear. Then, type in =SUM(cells to total). For example, the above formula would be: =SUM(B3..B7). *ClarisWorks* will automatically enter the cell addresses if you click and drag across the desired cells.

  • **Note:** *ClarisWorks* formulas will not work without the = sign.

3. To find the average, minimum, and maximum values, use these functions:

  =AVERAGE(cells)   =MIN(cells)   =MAX(cells)

  To use a formula over and over again in the same row or column:

  If you are creating a spreadsheet for multiple people or months, you may need to reuse your formulas. Instead of retyping them everytime, select Fill Right from the CALCULATE menu to go across or select Fill Down from the CALCULATE menu to go down.

Adding Borders

First, highlight the row header for the row you wish to give a border.

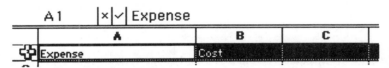

Second, the entire row should now be highlighted.

Third, select Borders from the Format menu. It will allow you to choose the part of the cell you wish to border. Select the desired border and click OK.

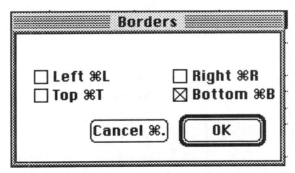

The row you highlighted should now have a solid line across the bottom.

	A	B	C	D	E
1	Expense	Cost			
2					
3	Pens	$6.50			
4	Pencils	$2.20			
5	Paper	$13.22			

HELPFUL FORMS AND PLANNING SHEETS

Once your students become comfortable being well-organized planners, they can use their own paper to plan. Until then, provide them with these guidelines for their technology projects.

Slide Show Storyboard

Use this form to plan for any type of slide show presentation. Copy the storyboard, front and back, for your students. Use as many sheets as necessary.

HyperStudio Planning Sheet

Help students create *HyperStudio* stacks with this versatile planning sheet.

HyperStudio Planning Web

Use these webs to help your students plan the organization and links of their *HyperStudio* presentation.

Publisher's Planning Sheet: Book Draft

Give your students the opportunity to arrange text and illustration in advance for a publishing project.

Status of the Class Project

Using this class list you can manage the progress of your students in any technology project.

Project Assessment

This rubric helps evaluate a student's project according to criteria set by you and your students and gives each student specific feedback.

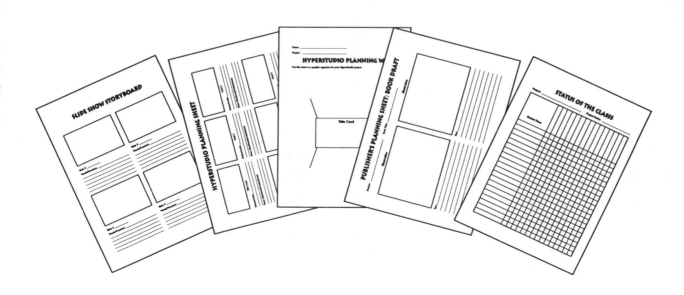

SLIDE SHOW STORYBOARD

Slide # _____

Words/Narration _____

_____

_____

_____

_____

_____

Slide # _____

Words/Narration _____

_____

_____

_____

_____

_____

Slide # _____

Words/Narration _____

_____

_____

_____

_____

_____

Slide # _____

Words/Narration _____

_____

_____

_____

_____

_____

HYPERSTUDIO PLANNING SHEET

Title Card

Buttons/Links: _____

Notes (Text/Sounds/Animations): _____

Card 1

Buttons/Links: _____

Notes (Text/Sounds/Animations): _____

Card 2

Buttons/Links: _____

Notes (Text/Sounds/Animations): _____

Card 3

Buttons/Links: _____

Notes (Text/Sounds/Animations): _____

Card 4

Buttons/Links: _____

Notes (Text/Sounds/Animations): _____

Card 5

Buttons/Links: _____

Notes (Text/Sounds/Animations): _____

Name: _____

Project: _____

HYPERSTUDIO PLANNING WEB

Use this sheet as a graphic organizer for your *HyperStudio* project.

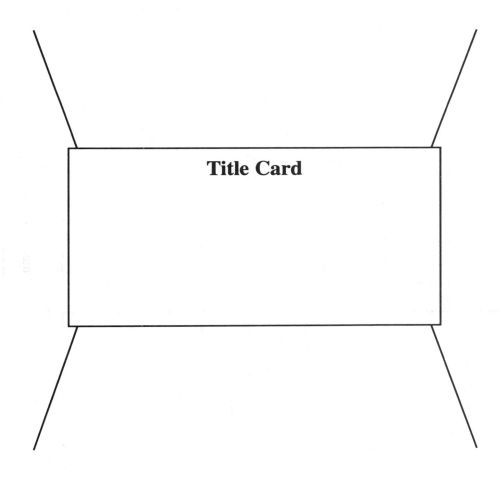

Title Card

PUBLISHER'S PLANNING SHEET: BOOK DRAFT

Student: _____

Book Title: _____

Illustration

Illustration

Text: _____

Text: _____

STATUS OF THE CLASSS

Project: _____   **Project Dates:** _____

Student Name														

SOFTWARE BIBLIOGRAPHY AND PURCHASE INFORMATION

ClarisWorks 4.0

ClarisWorks 4.0. Available from Claris Corporation. Claris Corporation, 5201 Patrick Henry Drive, Santa Clara, CA 95052.   1-800-544-8554.

ClarisWorks 4.0 is an integrated software package that combines word processing, drawing, painting, spreadsheets, database, and communications capabilities. There are no limits to the ways it can be used in the classroom for student and teacher productivity.

Teacher Note: Your school may already have software that will work well with the lesson plans in this book.

EasyBook

EasyBook. Available from Sunburst. Sunburst, 101 Castleton Street, P.O. Box 100, Pleasantville, NY 10570-0100. 1-800-321-7511.

This is an enjoyable and easy way to help your students become published authors. *EasyBook* makes it simple for students to publish and illustrate their own writings.

HyperStudio 3.0

HyperStudio 3.0. Available from Roger Wagner Publishing. Roger Wagner Publishing, Inc. 1050 Pioneer Way Suite P., El Cajon, California 92020. 1-800-421-6526.

HyperStudio is recommended for the ultimate in multimedia presentations. This program is easy to use and has dialogue boxes that appear throughout to help you create your projects, including graphics, sound, text, QuickTime movies, and video.

Kid Pix 2

Kid Pix 2. Available from Broderbund. Broderbund Software Direct, P.O. Box 6125 Novato, CA 94948-6125. 1-800-474-8840.

Kid Pix 2 is a very versatile program that allows students to create pictures, slide shows, and animations, as well as record sound.

The Writing Center

The Writing Center. Available from The Learning Company. The Learning Company, 6493 Kaiser Drive, Fremont, CA 94555. 1-800-852-2255.

This word processing/writing program is basic but very easy for students and teachers to use. The educational version comes with templates and sample projects for educational purposes.

OTHER SOFTWARE RESOURCES

Davidson and Associates

19840 Pioneer Ave.

Torrance, CA 90503

(800) 545-7677

Discis Knowledge Research, Inc.

P.O. Box 66

Buffalo, NY 14223-0066

(800) 567-4321

Edmark

P.O. Box 3218

Redmond, WA 98073-3218

(800) 426-0856

EduQuest/IBM

One Culver Road

Dayton, NJ 08810-9988

(800) 426-3327

Grolier Electronic Publishing

Sherman Turnpike

Danbury, CT 06816

(800) 356-5590

Lawrence Productions

1800 South 35th Street

Galesburg, MI 49053

(616) 665-7075

MECC

6160 Summit Drive North

Minneapolis, MN 55430-4003

(800) 685-6322

Microsoft Corproation

One Microsoft Way

Redmond, WA 98052

(800) 426-9400

National Geographic Educational Software

P.O. Box 98018

Washington, D.C. 20090-8018

(800) 368-2728

Scholastic, Inc.

2931 East McCarty Street

P.O. Box 7502

Jefferson City, MO 65102-9968

(800) 541-5513

Tom Snyder Productions

80 Coolidge Hill Road

Watertown, MA 02172

(800) 342-0236

Troll Associates

100 Corporate Drive

Mahwah, NJ 07498-0025

(800) 526-5289

TECHNOLOGY BOOKS AND RESOURCES

Barron, Ann E. and Gary W. Orwig. *New Technologies for Education—A Beginner's Guide.* Libraries Unlimited, 1995.

Bennett, Steve and Ruth. *The Official Kid Pix Activity Book.* Random House, 1993.

Chan, Barbara J. *Kid Pix Around the World—A Multicultural Computer Activity Book.* Addison Wesley, 1993.

Healey, Deborah. *Something to Do on Tuesday.* Athelstan, 1995.

Holmes, Kathleen and Don Rawitsch. *Evaluating Technology-Based Instructional Programs—An Educator's Guide.* Texas Center for Educational Technology, 1993.

Rathje, Linda, Jill Heyerly & Becky Schenck. *ClarisWorks for Students.* HRS Publication, 1995.

Reidl, Joan. *The Integrated Technology Classroom—Building Self-Reliant Learners.* Allyn & Bacon, 1995.

Sharp, Vicki F. *HyperStudio in One Hour.* ISTE, 1994.

Wetzel, Keith and Suzanne Painter. *Microsoft Works 3.0 for the Macintosh—A Workbook for Educators.* ISTE, 1994.

Willing, Kathlene R. and Suzanne Girard. *Learning Together—Computer Integrated Classrooms.* Pembroke Publishers Ltd., 1990.

Wodaski, Ron. *Absolute Beginner's Guide to Multimedia.* Sams Publishing, 1994.

Yoder, Sharon and David Moursund. *Introduction to ClarisWorks—A Tool for Personal Productivity.* ISTE, 1993.

Yoder, Sharon and Irene Smith. *Lookin Good! The Elements of Document Design for Beginners.* ISTE, 1995.

Magazines

The Computing Teacher
ISTE
1787 Agate Street
Eugene, Oregon 97043

MultiMedia Schools
462 Danbury Road
Wilton, CT 06897-9819

Technology and Learning
PO Box 49727
Dayton, Ohio 45449

Online Services

America Online, (800) 827-6364
CompuServe, (800) 848-8990
Classroom PRODIGY Service, (800) PRODIGY ext. 629
Netscape, (415) 254-1900